Theatre
on paper

This book and the exhibition were made possible through the generous assistance of the Howard Gilman Foundation, and the Samuel I. Newhouse Foundation, Inc.; as well as British Airways, the official airline of The Drawing Center.

A grant from the Andrew W. Mellon Foundation supported the publication of the catalogue.

Public funds from the National Endowment for the Arts also helped to make the exhibition and catalogue possible.

An Indemnity has been granted by the Federal Council on the Arts and Humanities.

Theatre on paper

Alexander Schouvaloff

Sotheby's Publications

Published in association with The Drawing Center, New York,
museum for the study and exhibition of drawings

© 1990 Alexander Schouvaloff

First published 1990 for Sotheby's Publications
by Philip Wilson Publishers Limited
26 Litchfield Street, London WC2H 9NJ
in association with The Drawing Center

ISBN 0 85667 373 0

LC 89-062229

Exhibition and catalogue organized by The Drawing
Center, museum for the study and exhibition of drawings,
35 Wooster Street, New York, NY 10013

All designs have been lent by the Board of Trustees,
Victoria and Albert Museum

Designed by Roy Cole
Typeset and printed by BAS Printers Limited, Over Wallop,
Hampshire
Bound by Hartnolls Limited, Bodmin, Cornwall

Contents

	Acknowledgements	6
	Preface by Martha Beck	7
	Note on the preface by Jeanne Thayer	7
	Author's preface	8
	Foreword by Sir John Gielgud	9
	Note on the foreword by Irene Worth	9
	Introduction	10
	Note on the Catalogue	17
The Catalogue	Set for a king	17
	Historical, regal and courtly costume	33
	Realism and reality	51
	Diagonal perspective	52
	Romantic realism	58
	Scenery built to architectural proportion	66
	The drawing-room comedy box	70
	The multiple set	74
	The composite set or abstract reality	76
	Plain and fancy dress	79
	Everyday and workaday costume	80
	Fantastical and fanciful	100
	Innovators	123
	Curtains and cloths	133
	Costume for dancers	140
	Male dancers in Diaghilev's Ballets Russes	140
	Ballerinas	152
	Furniture and properties	165
	Themes and variations	173
	Costumes for Gilbert and Sullivan operas	173
	Multiple costumes for groups, choruses and crowds	188
	Working it out	195
	Scene painting	204
	A poster, programmes and a petition	211
	Evocations	221
	Major exhibitions of theatre art in the twentieth century	233
	Select bibliography	236
	Biographical index of designers	240
	Photographic acknowledgements	244
	Index	245

To David Mayer
in gratitude

'It seems there is still very much to explain about the theatre, and The Art of the Theatre, before the world will understand rightly.'

Edward Gordon Craig, *Towards a New Theatre*

Acknowledgements

Many people have very kindly helped me in the preparation both of the exhibition and the catalogue. First and most important I thank Luciana Arrighi, Maria Björnson, John Bury, William Chappell, Alison Chitty, Jocelyn Herbert, David Hockney, Ralph Koltai, Tanya Moiseiwitsch, John Piper, Ronald Searle, Yolanda Sonnabend and Rouben Ter-Arutunian for generously allowing me to reproduce their designs. I am also especially grateful to Amanda Fielding who began as my assistant, to Julia Bigham who continued with great efficiency and good temper, and to Graham Brandon who took all the photographs of the designs with such sensitivity. I also appreciate the unstinting help given to me by Philip Dyer, Rhiannon Finamore, Wendy Fisher, James Fowler, Catherine Haill, Keith Lester, Leela Meinertas, Geraldine Morris, George Nash, Freddy Wittop and Sarah C. Woodcock and express my gratefulness to them. In particular I owe a huge debt of gratitude to Jane Bennett a most perceptive and delicately persuasive editor.

Finally, I thank Martha Beck for suggesting the exhibition in the first place and for her infectious enthusiasm, patience and continual support throughout the project.

Preface

Since opening in January 1977, The Drawing Center has sought through exhibitions and educational events to express the diversity, quality and importance of drawing – the creation of unique works on paper – as a major art form. Each year the Center presents five exhibitions. Those of an historical nature complement the Center's *Selections* series – group exhibitions of drawings by promising artists whose work is shown by the Center for the first time in New York. Each year over 2,500 artists show us their drawings. The Center exhibits drawings by architects, stage designers, film makers, sculptors and painters, and the process of choosing the artists is ongoing. Seven to eighteen artists are chosen for each exhibition. In the past thirteen years, 530 artists have been seen in forty-nine *Selections* exhibitions. Over a hundred are now in the collections of museums around the world. These exhibitions are special to the Center since every well-known artist was once promising and unknown.

Our first historical catalogue was *The Drawings of Antonio Gaudi* written by the distinguished architectural historian George R. Collins. Dr. Collins was also the author of *Visionary Drawings of Architecture and Planning*. Vincent Scully was the author of *The Travel Sketches of Louis I. Kahn*. John Harris, Jill Lever and Margaret Richardson were the authors of *Great Drawings from the Royal Institute of British Architects* and Otto Graf was the author of *Master Drawings of Otto Wagner*. Most recently John Harris and Gordon Higgott were the authors of *Inigo Jones: Complete Architectural Drawings*. Other exhibitions and catalogues for us have been: *Sculptors' Drawings Over Six Centuries* by Colin Eisler; *Reading Drawings: A Selection from the Victoria and Albert Museum* by Susan Lambert; *Drawings from Venice: Master Works from the Museo Correr* by Terisio Pignatti and Giandomenico Romanelli; *The Northern Landscape: Flemish, Dutch and British Drawings* from the Courtauld Collections by Dennis Farr and William Bradford; *The Art of Drawing in France 1400–1900: Master Drawings from the Nationalmuseum in Stockholm* by Per Bjurström; and, *Creative Copies: Interpretative Drawings from Michelangelo to Picasso* by Egbert Haverkamp-Begemann.

Drawings and projects for the theatre are in themselves sparkling entertainment. Alexander Schouvaloff has brilliantly selected these drawings, and arranged them into insightful groupings while skillfully elucidating their importance. The Drawing Center would like to extend gratitude to the Board of Trustees of the Victoria and Albert Museum for having lent us the works, and thus allowing the presentation of this exhibition and book.

From the Victoria and Albert Museum we would like to thank – Elizabeth Esteve-Coll, Director; John D. W. Murdoch, Assistant Director (Collections); Gwyn F. Miles, Surveyor of Collections; Susan B. Lambert and colleagues, Department of Designs, Prints and Drawings; John D. Wagstaff and colleagues in the Paper Conservation Department; Adrian Pasotti and Helen Shenton, Book Conservation Department; Nicky Edwards Smith and Graham Holden, Lettering and Mounting Department; Anne Buddle and colleagues, Registrar's Department; Ian Hodden-Brown and Malcolm Gordon, Packers; and Pat West. From the Theatre Museum: Dr. James Fowler, Julia Bigham, Graham Brandon, Amanda Fielding, Leela Meinertas, Sarah C. Woodcock, Wendy Fisher, and Catherine A. Haill.

Gratitude goes to the entire Board of Directors of The Drawing Center for their day-to-day support: Mrs. Walter N. Thayer and Michael Iovenko, Co-Chairman; Mrs. Felix G. Rohatyn, Vice-Chairman; Dita Amory, James M. Clark, Jr., Mrs. Colin Draper, Colin Eisler, Werner H. Kramarsky, Abby Leigh, William S. Lieberman, Mrs. Gregor W. Medinger, and Edward H. Tuck.

Members of the Advisory Board whom I would like to thank are Egbert Haverkamp-Begemann, John Langeloth, Loeb Professor of the History of Art at the Institute of Fine Arts, New York University; Per Bjurström, Director of the Nationalmuseum of Stockholm; Dennis Farr, Director of the Courtauld Galleries; John Harris, former Keeper of the Royal Institute of British Architects; C. Michael Kauffmann, Director of the Courtauld Institute; Giandomenico Romanelli, Director of the Civic Museums of Venice; Pierre Rosenberg, Conservateur en Chef, Louvre; and John Rowlands, Keeper of the Department of Prints and Drawings, British Museum.

Special thanks to my colleagues: Meryl Cohen, Registrar; Lena De Coursin, Administrative Assistant; Peter Gilmore, Director of Operations and Caroline Harris, Director of Development.

A personal note of thanks goes to Sir Colin Marshall, John Lampl, Lilla Santullo and the many members of the cargo crew and flight personnel of British Airways who have handled the shipping of very fragile drawings and the travel of couriers with skill, resourcefulness and unfailing courtesy.

Finally, I would like to thank the following people who helped in innumerable ways: Pierre Apraxine, David Bancroft, John Barelli, Michael Beirut, Jane Bennett, Huntington T. Block, William G. Bowen, Margaret Holben Ellis, Howard Gilman, Laura Hillyer, Anne Jackson, Heather Jones, Richard Oldenburg, Andrew Oliver, Richard Pribnow, Felix G. Rohatyn, Neil Rudenstine, Joline Tyhach, Lella and Massimo Vignelli, Alice Martin Whelihan, and Philip Wilson.

Martha Beck
Director, The Drawing Center

Note on the preface by The Drawing Center

The Board of Directors of The Drawing Center is pleased to present to the New York public this superb collection of drawings from the Victoria and Albert Theatre Museum in Covent Garden. It is both a fitting tribute to the long and justly famous history of the theatre in Britain and a further manifestation of the generosity of a great museum in sharing its treasures for the pleasure and benefit of its many admirers in the United States. We wish to add our thanks to Alexander Schouvaloff, the distinguished author of the superb catalogue, and to the administration and staff of the Victoria and Albert Museum, who have been thanked individually in the Foreword by Martha Beck, the founder and director of The Drawing Center.

Jeanne Thayer, Michael Iovenko
co-chairmen

Author's preface

Martha Beck of the Drawing Center suggested this exhibition. Later she gave me the title.

An exhibition has to have a purpose; it has to explore some idea, preferably some novel idea; it has to make an impact on the eye and, within certain definitions, should stimulate thought. I felt that an exhibition of drawings for the theatre, however wonderful they may be, arranged in chronological order, although possibly giving some insight into an historical development of the art of theatre, would ultimately not be very interesting. After all, every illustrated history of the theatre, and there are many, relies heavily upon set and costume designs for its illustrations and has them arranged in chronological sequence. So anyone just wanting to learn a little theatrical history should look at one of those books.

But an exhibition on the subject of theatre design itself would, I thought, be fascinating and illuminating from many points of view. Although the designs in this exhibition cover a period of three hundred and fifty years, its purpose is not historical but thematic. The sequential arrangement, therefore, is not chronological but is in a number of different groups of designs on the same theme. It shows that between 1608, the earliest design, and 1987, the latest, the problems of theatre design have often been solved in technically similar ways but that the imagination and inventiveness of designers is never-ending. The comparison of drawings in such an arrangement as this may also stimulate other designers and answer some curiosity in the layman about how things are ordered and made in the theatre. It also shows that although the art of the theatre is three-dimensional, set and costume designs are themselves an important means of expression and they have to be seen as works of art.

The production of a play in three acts with perhaps one scene and six different characters may need just as much thought on the part of the designer as an opera or ballet in four or five acts with four or five different scenes and several scores of singers or dancers, but the play may need just a few drawings whereas the opera or ballet may need several hundred. The Theatre Museum has an enormously rich and representative collection of European theatre design. I have selected 91 designs by 73 designers as being not only among the best in the collection by the greatest designers but also as being the best examples to explain the various themes. One drawing has to capture and conjure up the atmosphere of a whole production. Several times I have deliberately selected more than one design by the same designer in different groups, partly because I think they are very good designs but partly because they become familiar reference points from theme to theme. In my selection I have also stayed faithful to the name of the place of the exhibition – The Drawing Center: all the designs are unique drawings.

An exhibition should not be a book on walls, but this is the book of the exhibition. Both the exhibition and this book are an anthology, a select anthology of set and costume designs, which also includes quotations, observations and statements about the art and craft of theatre made by designers and writers, and excerpts from contemporary reviews by critics.

Foreword

I am of course delighted to be asked to contribute these few lines by way of introduction.

I have been tremendously attracted to costume and scenery ever since I first began to go to the theatre, and even hoped to design myself, before I decided to become an actor. Greatly influenced by the work of my second cousin, Edward Gordon Craig, I became, in the 20s, a great admirer of Claud Lovat Fraser, whose designs for *The Begger's Opera* and *As You Like It* in London, created an admiring public. I was also hugely impressed by the artists whom Diaghilev engaged to decorate his ballets (many of which I was fortunate enough to see) especially Benois and Bakst, Picasso, Derain and also by Bérard. When I began to direct for the theatre myself, I worked with a number of successively brilliant designers, including Motley, Mariano Andreu, Leslie Hurry, James Bailey, Cecil Beaton, and Oliver Messel, and found I could nearly always persuade them to incorporate many of my own ideas with their personally brilliant inventions – with extremely rewarding results.

In spite of the accuracy of photography, one is rarely given a very successful impression of the effect of stage decor on an audience. Drawings by the designers and, in some cases, the survival of models, as well as actual costumes, preserved after so many years, give one a far more fascinating record of past productions. It is absorbingly interesting to follow the progression of painted scenery and elaborately realistic costumes to the development of stage space and levels, a growing tendency towards simplification (even abstraction) and the use of modern materials and innovations, both of style and cut.

I have also followed America's brilliant designers with continued delight, among them Robert Edmond Jones, Jo Mielzener, Donald Oenslager, and many others. We should surely be able to look forward to mounting a similar exhibition to this one, but drawn from an American collection, so that England may also celebrate the brilliant achievements of the scene and costume designers of America over the generations.

John Gielgud   December 1989

Note on the foreword

The affinity between Actor and Designer is very great. Costumes become a point of inspiration for an actor, beyond the text, and each time the clothes of the character are put on, the Role becomes dominant. Everything else is discarded. The transformation is complete.

It is a privilege to have the Theatre Museum collection from the Victoria and Albert Museum available to us at The Drawing Center this year. Through the brilliant draughtsmanship of these designers, the great curtain parts and we enter a new world.

Irene Worth

Introduction

'... the purpose of playing, whose end, both at first and now, was and is, to hold, as 'twere, the mirror up to nature; to show virtue her own feature, scorn her own image, and the very age and body of the time his form and pressure. Now this overdone or come tardy off, though it make the unskilful laugh, cannot but make the judicious grieve; the censure of the which one must in your allowance o'erweigh a whole theatre of others.'
Hamlet, Act III scene 2

Hamlet's instruction to the First Player is true of all theatre. Theatre has to be convincing to work. A pact is made between the actors and the audience. The audience knows full well when it goes to the theatre that it is entering the world of make-believe, but it is silently sending a message to the actor 'Make me believe.' But convincing is not the same as real and the theatre is not like television where actors are mistaken for real people. An actor friend of mine who once appeared as a patient in a hospital bed for several episodes in a soap opera received many letters of sympathy and invitations to recuperate by the sea-side from well-intentioned viewers who were convinced by the realism on the screen. Reality in the theatre is different. It has to reflect life as it is inwardly felt not as it is outwardly lived. Theatre is the experience of real emotion.

The designer is one of the creators of that experience.

The theatre is a co-operative art. The designer works as one of a group but often in solitude. Any number of ideas may flow from the group but the designer has to crystallize them into a concrete and acceptable form. The success of his work, however, depends ultimately upon others, the craftsmen who make and paint his sets, cut and sew his costumes. The designer's work is always subject to compromise, so all the designer can do is try to ensure that the compromise is minimal – to do so he needs to have the right temperament. Bakst, for example, only found his true vocation when he began to work in the theatre. Although he used to complain about the frenzy of production, it provided him with the necessary adrenalin. Matisse, on the other hand, couldn't stand the hurly-burly and the fact that he could not have complete control however hard he tried. Dame Alicia Markova told me that when she appeared as a young girl in Stravinsky's *Le Chant du Rossignol* (*The Song of the Nightingale*) Matisse himself painted the designs on her costume while she was wearing it.

'The scene-designer remains what he has always been: one member of a group of interpreters. As such he must, usually in four weeks' time, construct a home or a palace, costume princes or paupers, transport any corner of the five continents or any one of a number of Arcadias to the theatre, provide any object that the actors must touch or handle, whether a throne or a kitchen chair, a dead sea-gull or the Sphinx, and out of paint, glue, canvas, gauze, wood and papier mâché create a world real enough to house the conflicts of human beings.'
Lee Simonson, *The Stage is Set*

'In order to do his best work as an artist, the designer should dominate and control the scene, yet, actually, he does his best work as an *artist of the theatre* when he is able to compromise and to co-operate with his fellow workers.'
Herman Rosse, 'The Stage Designer', *Theatre Arts Monthly*, May 1924

The theatre is a three-dimensional art. The designer is therefore an architect, or rather, he has to know about architecture. He has to know how to build sets and how they are painted, which is not the same thing as constructing buildings. Sets are full of tricks, that is illusions not trickery. The designer has to know about lighting, he has to be an art historian and know about the history of costume, but he must not be a slave to fashion or history. He has to have the eye of a sculptor and yet be able to paint and draw.

'A stage setting is not a background; it is an environment . . . The theatre demands of its craftsmen that they know their jobs. The theatre is a school. We shall never have done with learning. In the theatre as in life, we try first of all to free ourselves, as far as we can, from our own limitations. Then we can begin to practise this noble and magical "art". Then we may begin to dream.'
Robert Edmond Jones, *The Dramatic Imagination* quoted in programme of the Theatre Guild production of *Othello c.*1943.

'Ever since Sophocles reputedly invented scene painting, the designer of stage settings has been to a greater or less degree an interpreter of a playscript, primarily as an architect from the fifteenth through the eighteenth century, as a scene painter through most of the nineteenth century and since 1900 as an architect of stage space'.
Lee Simonson, *The Art of Scene Design*
—

A drawing for the theatre is a statement of an intention; it is an instruction to a craftsman; it is a unique document – often the only surviving visual record of a performance.

The invention of photography has not lessened the lasting value of a drawing for the theatre, any more than it has affected the intrinsic value of any work of art.

Some designers only make drawings, some designers only make models, some make both. Models get damaged or broken in the scenic workshops; drawings also disappear.

'What a tremendous distance there is between the scenic dream of an artist or a stage designer and its realization upon the stage.'
Constantin Stanislavsky, *My Life in Art*

A drawing for the theatre is a work of art.
—

Most designers seem to agree about the purpose of design and the role of the designer. He is there as one of a team to support the actor by creating the right, that is the true, the real space in which he can bring the text to life.

Most of the designs in this exhibition were made for theatres with proscenium arches ('picture frame' stages) but then most theatres since the seventeenth century have been built with prosceniums. Lately designers have tried to ignore the arch by bringing the set out over the orchestra pit and into the auditorium. This creates a distortion in the architecture, and the sightlines for spectators in the circle and galleries are then usually obscured. During the last twenty years or so architects, at the behest of directors, have built a number of theatres without proscenium arches (the Octagon in Bolton, the Crucible in Sheffield, the Exchange in Manchester, the Olivier in London are some examples). Some directors, rather than the audiences I suspect, have a theory that a close rapport between actor and spectator can only be achieved on an open stage and when the two are close together. In my experience, if they are too close the audience becomes involuntarily embarrassed. Since, however, most theatres still have proscenium arches, people will continue to go to theatres with them.

The problem is Shakespeare. His own theatre was so different and unique to England. Scholars have long argued and will no doubt long continue to argue about what exactly the Globe Theatre was like. We do know, however, that the 'Wooden O' (as Shakespeare called his theatre in *Henry V*) was probably an octagonal building and had seven separate acting areas on three levels. On the first level was the Platform (open apron stage) flanked by entrances on each side with the Study behind; on the second level was the Tarras (terrace or balcony) with the Chamber behind flanked by window stages on each side; on the third level was the Musicians' Gallery. The audience was arranged in tiered galleries round five of the eight sides of the octagon and standing in the Yard (pit). It was thrilling to discover during the excavations of the Rose Theatre in 1989 that it could have held three thousand people (a thousand more than The Royal Opera House, Covent Garden), and that they ate hazelnuts in the pit. The rapid change of scene in time and place was no problem for Shakespeare's theatre, but designers doing his plays in proscenium theatres have always had to make a special compromise.

Most recently there has been a spate of productions where directors, with the connivance of designers, have deliberately shown off and re-set operas and plays in time and place, thereby going completely against the text. The result is a falsehood and a betrayal. It *can* work sometimes, but it is a very delicate matter. Shakespeare and Verdi seem to suffer the vanity of directors more than most, but they will survive and do.

The playwright, the composer, and the choreographer need the designer in order to succeed in the theatre – they need the third dimension.

—

The director also needs the designer. (Sometimes the director is also the designer, but that is quite rare.) Progress towards the fulfilment of an idea is livelier and more fruitful when it is not made in isolation because one idea leads to another more easily. The director may only have a blurred picture in his mind of what the set should look like, the designer then goes away and puts it into focus with sketches and models. Eventually the 'environment for the actors' is agreed upon. The designer then makes final sketches, detailed models, working drawings, and ground plans and supervises the work of transforming them into sets and costumes. It sounds simple. It is better organised today than before.

'In London, with but one or two exceptions, a theatrical production is a chaotic affair knit together only by the forceful personality of the producer (now termed director) . . . His first act is to meet the author and gather his views on the representation of the play . . . The producer's second act is to commission A to paint scenery, B to design dresses, C to write music and D to stage manage. Now A will paint his scenery in Lambeth, B will design his dresses in Chelsea, C will write his music in Hertfordshire, and D, who is incidentally responsible for all "properties" and lighting, will buy furniture in Tottenham Court Road. None of these people will meet each other until a week or so before production, when a dress rehearsal is called. The result is, of course, muddle – dresses, scenery, music and detail are contradictory and at variance.'
Claud Lovat Fraser, 'The Art of the Theatre', *The Studio*, 15 November 1921.

But some people, like Fraser, have always taken theatre design seriously.

The first two groups of the exhibition concentrate on 'historical' or traditional designs for historical or classic plays.

The drawing by Parigi [No. 1] is not only the earliest design in the show, 1608, but also the only known complete drawing by this important artist. It shows how settings began by fixing the stage on a central perspective. The symmetrical set is most appropriate for ballet (*Don Quixote* by Edward Burra [No. 5], *Nocturne* by Sophie Fedorovitch [No. 6]) where an empty floor is needed for the dancers or for fanciful operas (*Tiresias* by Osbert Lancaster [No. 7]) where plausibility is created from pastiche. Symmetry is also an appropriate basis for a permanent structure with minor changes of set for each change of scene. This is particularly true for productions of Shakespeare's plays in proscenium theatres. His scenes succeed one another rapidly and the audience's attention and involvement in the action will flag if they are frequently kept waiting in the dark for complicated set changes to take place. A symbolic basic structure (Georges Wakhevitch's *Hamlet* [No. 4]) provides a necessary visual continuity. A designer has to consider the overall colour effect of each scene, that is the effect of the colour of the costumes worn by the players within the set. A curious thing happens in a large theatre. From a certain distance the actor in costume can appear to be two-dimensional and merge with the set. The designer has to guard against this optical illusion. All costume, therefore, has to 'read' easily in the theatre, even from great distances. Historical costume, while perhaps being based on authenticity, need not be historically accurate, as for example the Prince in *Cendrillon* by Natalia Gontcharova [No. 13] or Queen Elizabeth I in *Gloriana* by John Piper [No. 14]. Designers follow their own fantasies for revue (Laurence Irving for *A Venetian Wedding* [No. 11]) and pre-history (Roger Furse for *King Lear* [No. 15]). Alexandre Benois (courtiers in *Le Pavillon d'Armide* [No. 10], a woman and child in the crowd in *Petrushka* [No. 33], or Petrushka himself [No. 54]) is a real, though always charming, traditionalist not only in style but also in manner.

———

The next groups [Nos 16–36] show how designers have approached the problem of creating reality on the stage by means of theatrical realism. Everybody knows that an actor going out of a french window into a garden is not actually doing so, that the window has no glass and that the flowers in the garden are not real. Even eating a steak or ironing a shirt on stage doesn't fool the audience into thinking it is watching actual life. Designers have had to invent a number of conventions in the design of their sets so that, first of all, the actor can feel secure in them and, once this is achieved, then the audience can believe in the invented reality. A realistic set can be romantic (*Giselle* by James Bailey [No. 20]), or magical (*Jack and the Beanstalk* by Robert Caney [No. 21]), cut-away (*The Old Ladies* by Reece Pemberton [No. 25]), or architecturally impossible (*The Skin of Our Teeth* by Roger Furse [No. 26]). Realistic clothes not only have to look real but they must also be practical, because the performer has to feel comfortable. A dancer has to be able to dance (a huntsman in *Giselle* by James Bailey [No. 29]), a singer has to be able to sing (General Kutuzov in *War and Peace* by Mstislav Dobujinsky [No. 31], Little Buttercup in *HMS Pinafore* by George Sheringham [No. 32]).

———

Fantasy is the designer's dream world [Nos 37–46]. His imagination is bounded only by practicality and fidelity to the text. But he may dream of things the author never dreamt of. The designer, as always, gives fantasy a third dimension.

French revue is fantasy of a special, and particularly seductive, kind. There are four designs by supreme masters of the art: Erté for Prince Assad in *L'Orient Merveilleux ou 1002 Nuits de Bagdad* [No. 42], Dany for an American girl in *Femmes en Folie* [No. 43], Brunelleschi for *Schéhérazade* [No. 44] and Gesmar for Dewar's white label whisky in *Mieux que Nue!* [No. 45].

'Generally speaking, I was always guided by two principles. The first was to find one detail (hairstyle, jewellery or some other accessory) which was sufficiently interesting or striking to suggest the idea of a costume. The second was to build a costume by extending the lines of the naked body into decorative arabesques. Of course, those days you had more to dress on the nude – they wear far less these days, in the eighties.'
Erté quoted by Charles Castle, *The Folies Bergère*

—

Innovators in the theatre are necessary because it is only through them that the art of theatre progresses. There are technical innovations such as the invention of moveable and changeable scenery, gas and electric light, revolving stages and hydraulic lifts, which give people ideas about the practice of theatre, but then there are also people who, accepting the technicalities, have ideas about the art of theatre. These are the true innovators because they are concerned with the very nature of the art. Their theatre is not necessarily popular or commercial, although it can be both. It is almost an axiom that what is experimental for one generation is commonplace for the next. In all art, including the art of the theatre, some people write the rules and then others come along to break them; it is called progress. All histories of the theatre are defined by the succession of innovators, but, as I said in the preface, the purpose of this book is not to be a history of the theatre. Here is a small group of four designs by artists who have written new rules and broken old ones. Sometimes innovators are designers who are also directors and actors (Edward Gordon Craig [No. 47]), sometimes they are primarily designers (Ralph Koltai [No. 50]), more often they are directors working with designers (Max Reinhardt with Ernst Stern [No. 48] and Alexander Tairov with Alexandra Exter [No. 49]), rarely are they actors.

Innovators provide the occasional burst of required oxygen; they prevent stagnation and death. Art, and the art of theatre, only survives by leaps of the imagination being given a practical application.

—

One form of theatre design that is purely two-dimensional is for painted cloths. There are three quite different examples of this art in the next group: Leslie Hurry's cloth for *Swan Lake* [No. 51], Claud Lovat Fraser's for *As You Like It* [No. 52] and Tanya Moiseiwitsch's for *Peter Grimes* [No. 53], a ballet, a play and an opera.

The Russian group of artists known as *Mir Iskusstva* (*The World of Art*), founded by Alexandre Benois [Nos 10, 33, 54], Léon Bakst [Nos 55, 65, 74], Serge Diaghilev and others, began by producing a glossy magazine of the same name edited by Diaghilev in 1898. They went on to arrange art exhibitions including an influential exhibition of Russian art in Paris in 1906. Diaghilev then produced seasons of opera and ballet and, from 1909 until 1929, ballet only. This was the revolutionary Ballets Russes. For twenty years the company toured Europe and North and South America but never performed in Russia. It had an enormous international influence on the art of the theatre. Under Diaghilev's inspiration the Ballets Russes not only revived but also transformed many ideas of design for the theatre. The painter with an unrestrained palette of sensual colour came to the stage and the theatre was never the same again. Bakst is generally recognised as being the greatest of Diaghilev's designers; it was he who transformed fashion as well as theatre; it was his ballets which created instant but lasting sensations. Diaghilev then enticed other painters to the theatre as illustrated here by Picasso, with drawings for his first production *Parade* [No. 56], Juan Gris, with a costume design for *Daphnis and Chloé* [No. 57], and Giorgio de Chirico, with a costume design for *Le Bal* [No. 58].

'It was no accident that what was afterwards known as the *Ballets Russes* was originally conceived not by the professionals of the dance, but by a circle of artists, linked together by the idea of Art as an entity. Everything followed from the common desire of several painters and musicians to see the fulfilment of the theatrical dreams which haunted them; but I emphasise again that there was nothing *specific* or *professional* in their dreams. On the contrary, there was a burning craving for Art in general.'
Alexandre Benois, *Reminiscences of the Russian Ballet*

Ballet is about bodies and especially about legs: it therefore needs a conventional dress for the dancer which shows them off to best advantage. The suitable dress was developed during the nineteenth century when the diaphanous calf-length skirt was raised until it became the rigid tutu. Paul Nash kept to the established tradition in his designs for Tamara Karsavina in *The Truth about the Russian Dancers* [No. 60]. Now the skirt is soft again as designed by Christian Bérard for *Symphonie Fantastique* [No. 62], William Chappell for *Les Patineurs* [No. 63] and Yolanda Sonnabend for *Swan Lake* [No. 64].

——

The next groups [Nos 65–81] are concerned with different practical aspects of design.

As well as sets and costumes, the designer is responsible for the furniture (Bakst for *Le Spectre de la Rose* [No. 65]) and 'properties' (Audrey Cruddas for *Macbeth* [No. 66]), or the objects used by the actors. Sometimes these are bought from antique shops, sometimes they come from a theatre store, but usually they have to be made for the production because nothing else will fit in with the designer's scheme.

The D'Oyly Carte opera company who produced the operas of Gilbert and Sullivan always insisted on a certain prescribed formula and the designers engaged by them for new productions had to maintain the original spirit. The costume variations for the same character in two widely different operas (Nanki-Poo in *The Mikado* and Casilda in *The Gondoliers* [Nos 67–73]) show how designers over the years maintained the spirit but added their own spice.

The designer, as I have said before, is always concerned with the total visual effect. Sometimes many costumes have to be the same (as Bakst's for sixteen cake-walkers in a revue *Hullo, Tango!* [No. 74]), sometimes only similar (as Dobujinsky's for a chorus in *War and Peace* [No. 75], or Thomas's townsmen in *Gismonda* [No. 76]).

Writers think in words, but sometimes in pictures, for example Isaac Pocock visualizing one of his scenes in *King Arthur* [No. 77]; artists think in pictures on paper (the anonymous artist working out a scene at the Folies Bergère [No. 78], or Maria Björnson working out costumes for *A Midsummer Night's Dream* [No. 79], or John Piper sketching sets for *Don Giovanni* [No. 81]); scene painters have to work things out on paper first (Alexandre Schervashidze squaring up a drawing [No. 80]). The mind's eye alone is not reliable enough.

I have also included three designs and one drawing which are not set or costume designs. They are, nevertheless, an essential part of theatre. Programmes (by Dudley

Hardy for Bertram Mills' Circus [No. 82], by Pavel Tchelitchew for Diaghilev's Russian Ballet season [No. 83], and by Ronald Searle for a pantomime in a prisoner-of-war camp [No. 84]) are the permanent record of ephemeral performances. Without them we would not know what had taken place, where or when, nor would we know who had taken which part. Without them, therefore, there would be no theatre history. Programmes are the backbone of any theatre collection. There is also in this group a drawing made by David Hockney for a petition [No. 85] to save the Theatre Museum.

——

And in the last section there are six drawings for the memory. I have called them 'evocations'. The first is by a sculptor, Barbara Hepworth [No. 86], the others are by painters who have also worked in the theatre, Ceri Richards [No. 87], Rouben Ter-Arutunian [No. 88], Michel Larionov [No. 89], Antoni Clavé [No. 90] and Bernard Meninsky [No. 91]. They are, to my mind, supremely expressive of the intention of the artist and therefore successfully evoke the nature of the pieces for which they are designs. It is not really significant that these drawings are for operas and ballets; I could equally well have chosen six other designs from previous groups.

'The scenic setting has a distinct mission in theatrical life – and but one mission. That is so to express the purpose, the spirit, the symbolism of the play as to enhance and intensify its character.'
John Wenger, 'The Mission of the Stage Setting' in *American Stage Designs* catalogue, 1919

——

Design in the theatre has now come full circle.

Gods ascending and descending on clouds, magical scenic transformations transporting mortals from one continent to another on apparently real seas with rolling waves have become roller-skaters in *Starlight Express*, phantoms at the opera or Laurence Olivier as a hologram. The mechanical inventions of the Renaissance court theatres have become the electronic, high-tech gadgets of contemporary popular musical theatre.

It's the tricks that count not the text. 'Go and see *Metropolis* for the set,' they said, 'but there is no need to stay for the show.'

Reality is left behind. But the real theatre will survive.

I sometimes think that the most successful design in the theatre is one that is not noticed by the critics and arouses no comment from the audience. One designer, at least, agrees with me. Jocelyn Herbert [No. 39] said: 'If your set is applauded when the curtain goes up, you've gone too far.'

——

When all is said and done the theatre is also an industry.

Set for a king

As described in the preface this book is arranged in groups of designs.

The production details relate to the particular design and are therefore, not necessarily the details of the first production. All theatres are in London unless otherwise stated. The dates given are those of the 'official' first performance and therefore ignore any 'try-out' or preview performances which may or may not have taken place.

All works are on paper unless otherwise stated.

Measurements are given in millimetres, height before width.

References under 'literature' only include direct references to the particular drawing; they do not include references to reviews of the production in newspapers and magazines.

Quotations from reviews in the notes that follow the catalogue entries are from newspapers published in London unless otherwise stated.

The invention of the proscenium or 'picture frame' stage with a curtain led to the development of elaborate, moveable scenery and the use of perspective in symmetrical settings. The vanishing point defined the best seat in the house.

In the palace grounds at Drottningholm in Sweden there is a perfectly preserved theatre which was built for the Swedish royal family in 1766. In its auditorium and stage, with its many sets of eighteenth-century scenery, we can fortunately still see exactly what early proscenium theatres were like. In *Theatre Arts Monthly*, April 1924, John Mason Brown described this theatre: 'To enter the auditorium of the Drottningholm theatre, with its cream colored walls, painted decorations, and tiers of blue benches rising steadily toward the back away from the raised thrones of the King and Queen, and to look through the deep proscenium at the old stage, where one of the original settings is in place, is to be carried back with complete illusion into the world of a hundred and fifty years ago . . . The Court theatres of the eighteenth century were no democratic institutions – a fact made amusingly clear by the very arrangement of the seats. The auditorium which is without a balcony is laid out with a rigid sense of social distinction. Behind the orchestra pit in the small rounded part of the auditorium which narrows down into a rectangle one-third of the way back are the thrones of the King and Queen.'

Proscenium theatres are now laid out with a rigid sense of financial distinction but while they continue to be used symmetrical scenery will be designed for the best seat in the house.

The drawings in this first section show how designers have used the convention of symmetry.

Il Giudizio di Paride (The Judgement of Paris)

A pastoral entertainment by Michelangelo Buonarotti, the younger
Uffizi Palace, Florence,
25 October 1608

1
Giulio Parigi
(1571–1635)

Set design for the fourth intermezzo: The ship of Amerigo Vespucci on the shores of the Indies
Pen and ink
317 × 425
(S.295–1978)

Provenance
Lorna Lowe Gallery, London

Exhibitions
London, National Book League, *Old Master Drawings*, 23 June–9 July 1976, No. 22
Hanover, New Hampshire, Dartmouth College Museum & Galleries, *Theater Art of the Medici*, 10 October–7 December 1980, No. 23
London, Victoria and Albert Museum, *Images of Show Business*, 17 November 1982–17 April 1983, No. 56

Literature
Clifford, Timothy, 'Old Master Drawings in London,' *The Burlington Magazine*, vol. 118, (London, August 1976), p. 609, fig. 74, p. 611
Blumenthal, Arthur R., *Theater Art of the Medici*, [catalogue], (Hanover, 1980), pp. 49–53, ill. p. 52
Fowler, James (editor), *Images of Show Business*, (London, 1982), ill. no. 56
Strong, Roy, *Art and Power*, (Woodbridge, Suffolk, 1984), pp. 149–52, ill. no. 101

Late sixteenth- and early seventeenth-century Florentine festivals and *intermezzi* are of great significance in the development of stage scenery and effects. The chief designer responsible for the most inventive, original and spectacular court festivities of the Medici was Bernardo Buontalenti (1536–1608). The side-pieces in his designs are thought by some scholars not to be genuine 'wings', (painted canvas flats sliding in and out on grooves) but *telari*, that is three-sided prisms imitating classical *periaktoi* which can swivel to reveal different scenes.

Parigi was a pupil of Buontalenti and it is therefore probable that he used the same system for his side-pieces. This is the only-known, original and complete set design by Parigi, although many contemporary etchings based on his drawings exist.

Il Giudizio di Paride was written for the festivities celebrating the wedding of Prince Cosimo Medici and Maria Maddalena, Arch-Duchess of Austria. This scene, changing history, shows Amerigo Vespucci discovering America.

2
attributed to Ferdinando
Galli da Bibiena
(1657–1743)

Design for a permanent set
Executed *c*.1740
Pen and ink with grey wash, laid
down on card
Card inscribed 'Ferdin. Bibiena
architecte 1697 + 1743/Ecole
Bolonaise/Perspective de Théâtre'
325 × 505
(S.85–1982)

Provenance
Sotheby's, London

Working all over Europe, but especially in Vienna, members of the Galli family from Bibiena exerted one of the strongest influences upon scenery during the baroque period. Ferdinando (1657–1743) and Francesco (1659–1739) continued a tradition started by their father Giovanni Maria (1619–65). They were succeeded by Ferdinando's sons Alessandro (1687–*c*.1769), Giuseppe (1696–1757), Antonio (1700–74) and Giovanni Maria (*c*.1704–69). Giuseppe's son Carlo (1728–87) was also a famous theatrical designer. The whole family worked in such a similar style that it is often difficult to attribute individual drawings. Their great scenic innovation was the introduction of diagonal perspective, and perspective with two vanishing points (see No. 16). This design is attributed to Ferdinando but it could be by Giuseppe.

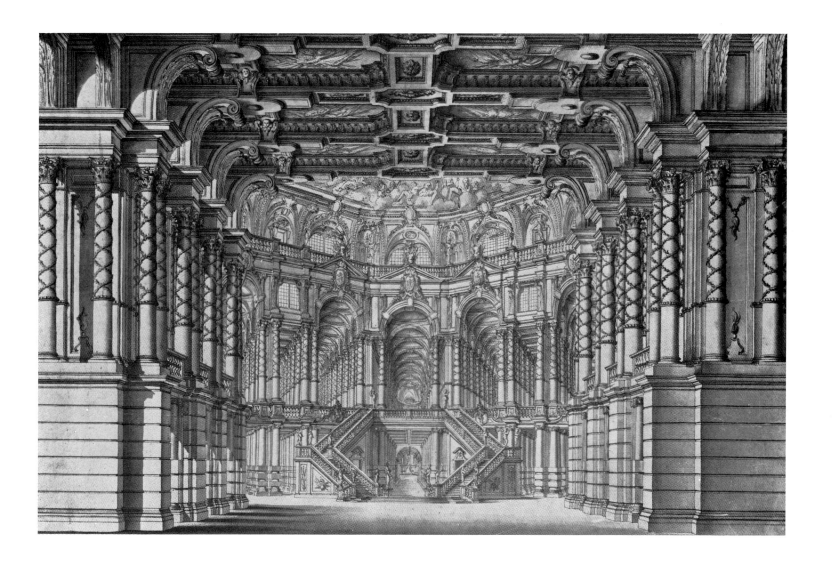

The Cenci

Play in two parts and ten scenes by
Percy Bysshe Shelley
Director: Michael Benthall
Designer: Leslie Hurry
Composer: John Lambert
Principals:
Count Francesco Cenci:
Hugh Griffith
Beatrice, Daughter to Cenci:
Barbara Jefford
Orsino, a prelate: John Phillips
Lucretia, wife to Cenci and step-
mother to his children:
Veronica Turleigh
Old Vic Theatre, 29 April 1959

3

Leslie Hurry

(1909–78)

Set design for Part II scene 4: A Hall
of Justice, Rome
Pencil, pen and ink, and
watercolour
305 × 483
(S.2207–1986)

Provenance
Given by The British Council

'. . . There might have been something eerily powerful as well as histrionically picturesque if an Italianate vein had been pursued. The production is as Italian as Buckingham Palace.'
The Observer, 3 May 1959

This is not necessarily a comment on the designer who is not mentioned by name in any review. The castle is S. Angelo in Rome. By placing it off-centre Leslie Hurry avoids total symmetry and creates a more credible atmosphere without losing a severe formality.

Hamlet
by William Shakespeare
Director: Peter Brook
Designer: Georges Wakhevitch
Composer: Thomas Eastwood
Principals:
Hamlet: Paul Scofield
Claudius: Alec Clunes
Gertrude: Diana Wynyard
Ophelia: Mary Ure
Moscow Art Theatre (Filial
Theatre), 23 November 1955
Phoenix Theatre, 8 December 1955

4

Georges Wakhevitch

(1907–84)

Design for the permanent set
Pencil and gouache on canvas board
Signed Wakhewitch/London 1950
362 × 457
(S.1271–1986)

Provenance
The artist's estate
Mme Million Jutheau, Paris
Bought with funds given by the
Theatre Museum Association

'In the old tradition of Shakespearian travelling companies the setting, designed, like the costumes, by Mr Georges Wakhevitch, was simple and one basic set was used throughout the three acts in which the play was presented. By the skilful lighting and the addition of cannon, red hangings or the piles of a pier Wakhevitch has managed effectively to suggest the change of scene from ramparts to throne-room or quayside, and these ingenious shifts were several times applauded.'
The Times, 25 November 1955, on the performance in Moscow

'Elsinore, apparently, was shaped like a birdcage built of rather dirty reinforced concrete. Very symbolic. A suitable place for Hamlet's imprisoned soul. But extremely uncomfortable to look at and, I imagine, hell to live in – whoever was king.'
Derek Monsey, *Daily Express*, 11 December 1955

I can only think that because the date is wrong, Wakhevitch signed this design much later, perhaps for an exhibition, and no longer remembered when he drew it.

Don Quixote

Ballet in five scenes
Composer: Roberto Gerhard
Conductor: Constant Lambert
Choreographer: Ninette de Valois
Designer: Edward Burra
Principals:
Don Quixote: Robert Helpmann
Sancho Panza: Alexander Grant
The Lady Dulcinea:
Margot Fonteyn
The Sadler's Wells Ballet Company
Royal Opera House, Covent Garden,
20 February 1950

5

Edward Burra

(1905–76)

Set design for scene 4: The Cave of
Montesinos
Pencil, watercolour, laid on card
518 × 680
(S.2115–1986)

Provenance
Given by The British Council

'For admirers of Edward Burra there are three fine settings and three startling curtains,
typical works, wild in design, perverse in drawing, hard in colour.'
The Observer, 26 February 1950

Nocturne

Ballet in one scene by Edward
Sackville-West
Composer: Frederick Delius ('Paris')
Conductor: Constant Lambert
Choreographer: Frederick Ashton
Designer: Sophie Fedorovitch
Principals:
A Spectator: Frederick Ashton
A Young Man: Robert Helpmann
A Rich Girl: Pamela May
A Poor Girl: Margot Fonteyn
Vic-Wells Ballet Company
Princes Theatre, (now Shaftesbury)
28 November 1944

6

Sophie Fedorovitch

(1893–1953)

Set design
Pencil, watercolour and gouache
Signed in pencil S. Fedorovitch
sheet 375 × 515, image 290 × 430
(S.538–1980)

Provenance
John Carr-Doughty

Exhibition
London, Victoria and Albert
Museum, *Sophie Fedorovitch*, from
5 December 1955 and subsequently
toured by Circulation Department
during 1956, no. 31a

Literature
Hogben, Carol (editor), *Sophie
Fedorovitch*, [catalogue], (London,
1955)

The first performance of the ballet was at the Sadler's Wells Theatre on 10 November 1936. Delius described his *Paris* as a nocturne, and the programme note said 'it is this aspect of the music, rather than the purely local aspect, that has been stressed by the artists responsible for the present production. They have made no attempt at a realistic evocation of Paris itself.' *The Times* critic described the ballet: 'Against the simplest architectural setting the dancers enact a little drama that is commonplace enough in itself – the conflict between a rich girl and a poor flower-seller for the love of a young man.' *The Daily Telegraph* noted that 'the décor was pleasingly open to the dancing line.'

This design is for the revival of the ballet in 1944 at the Princes Theatre. It was repeated at Covent Garden in 1946 but the set did not stretch satisfactorily to the larger stages and the ballet was withdrawn from the repertoire at Sophie Fedorovitch's request.

Tiresias

Comic opera in two acts with
prologue and entr'acte
Based on the play *Les Mamelles de
Tirésias* (*The Breasts of Tiresias*) by
Guillaume Apollinaire
Composer: Francis Poulenc
Conductor: Charles Mackerras
Pianos: Francis Poulenc and
Benjamin Britten
Director: John Cranko
Designer: Osbert Lancaster
Principals:
Thérèse: Jennifer Vyvyan
Her Husband: Peter Pears
Jubilee Hall, Aldeburgh, 13 June
1958 (First performance in England
as part of the Aldeburgh Festival)

7

Osbert Lancaster

(1908–86)

Design for Act 1 and 2: The Square
of Zanzibar, an imaginary town on
the French Riviera, somewhere
between Nice and Monte Carlo
1910
Pencil, pen and ink and gouache
Signed Osbert Lancaster
326 × 545 overall (four sheets pasted
together: border, two wings,
backcloth)
(Circ.740–1967)

Provenance
Wright Hepburn Gallery, London
Circulation Department, Victoria
and Albert Museum

Historical, regal and courtly costume

For gods and kings, queens and courtiers

In a series of four dialogues, quoted by Nagler in *A Source Book in Theatrical History*, Leone di Somi (1527–92), casting himself as Veridico, developed his theories of stagecraft including costume: 'Veridico: I make efforts to dress the actors always in as noble a fashion as is possible for me, but in such a manner that there is a sense of proportion among them, in view of the fact that the rich costume . . . particularly in these times when pomp is at its highest peak, adds much reputation and beauty to comedies, and even more to tragedies.'

Before a true sense of history established itself in people's minds in the nineteenth-century, historical costume in the theatre just meant something that looked as if it had been worn a long time ago, and was usually based on imaginary ideas of Roman costume. David Garrick (1717–79) played Shakespearean parts in his own contemporary clothes with only minor adjustments and suggestive details of another period to pin-point the individual character. He did not, for example, dress himself up as a Scotsman to play Macbeth. It was Charles Kean, in the 1850s, whose obsession with historical accuracy established a tradition of dressing an historical play which has for the most part been maintained ever since.

—

'The requirements of his (the designer's) craft are those of any other graphic art: a sense of line as embodied particularly in a feeling for drapery and pattern; a sense of colour made more practical by a knowledge of the effects of stage lights upon it and more significant by a feeling for the emotional and symbolic values of colour; invention and originality; and to balance them, a knowledge of and understanding of the past, useful in every art as a source of fresh inspiration, and as a check to extravagances, and necessary to this art in particular where an accurate representation both of archaeological detail and of the general spirit of a bygone age are so frequently demanded.'
Sir Barry Jackson, 'Costume' in G. Sheringham and M. Morrison *Robes of Thespis*

'And "costume plays" are frequently sacrificed, on the one hand, to archaeological academism and on the other to mere luridness of colour or extravagance of design. And when success is achieved in regard to costume *or* setting, how seldom again do *both* concur to produce complete illusional harmony.'
Charles B. Cochran, 'Stage Decoration and Fantasy', *The Studio*, December 1927

'The scenic art reflects to a greater degree than other graphic arts contemporary modes and manners. The greatest designer of stage costumes may unconsciously echo the prevailing style of the coutouriers (*sic*). The waist line dictated by Paris in the 1920s was often reflected in the robes of a Herod or a Richard II in a contemporary production.'
Laurence Irving, introduction to catalogue *George W. Harris* (Liverpool 1958, see No. 19)

33

suyuant le desseny

196

2. cauallien qui accompa
tripolin

prince le tertolly

2. suinant Apollo
au ballet de phorbas

prenost &Tarraube

Ballet du Roy (often known as *Ballet d'Apollon*)

Verses by Théophile de Viau
Composer: Antoine Boësset
Performers included Louis XIII of France and Duc de Luynes (the King's favourite)
Louvre, Paris, 18 February 1621

8

Studio of Daniel Rabel

(active 1613–34)

Costume design for Prévost and Tarraube as Followers of Apollo in the Phorbas' Ballet
Pen and ink, and watercolour
Inscribed 'suyvant le desseing' ('follow the drawing'), '2 suivant Apollo au ballet de phorbas' ('2 followers of Apollo in the ballet of the Phorbas'), 'prevost & Tarraube', numbered '196'
265 × 185
(S.1142–1986)

Provenance
Sotheby's, London
Purchased with assistance from the National Art-Collections Fund

Exhibition
London, Theatre Museum, *The King's Pleasures – newly discovered designs for the Court Ballet of Louis XIII*, 24 April–2 August 1987

Literature
Margaret M. McGowan, *The Court Ballet of Louis XIII*, (London, 1987), ill. no. 25

This design and others from the same studio (for a pastry cook [No. 27], for an old man [No. 36], for a dog [No. 37], and for a headless character [No. 46]) are from a collection of 188 designs which was discovered a few years ago in a private library in Germany. They are by various hands but all come from the studio of Daniel Rabel who worked for the French Court of Louis XIII between 1613 and 1634. They are also annotated by different people with instructions and the names of the persons portraying the parts. Rabel is especially remarkable for his liveliness and inventiveness. The Theatre Museum acquired forty-five drawings and more research is needed to distinguish the different artists.

The convention of drawing a costume design was established early and did not really change until the twentieth century. Even now, many designers maintain the traditional style.

Atys
Lyrical tragedy
Composer: Jean-Baptiste Lully
Librettist: Philippe Quinault
1676

9
Jean-Louis Berain
(1637–1711)

Costume design for Hercules
Watercolour
375 × 235
(S.1108–1982)

Provenance
Pierre Cornette de Saint Cyr

A rather effete version of the hero of Greek and Roman mythology. He is holding his club and wearing his traditional lion's skin but the rest of his costume is 'heroic' seventeenth-century Roman. This design shows clearly the established symbolism of costume design for ballet which was defined by Father Claude-François Ménestrier in his *Des Ballets Anciens et Modernes* (1681) where he writes: 'The first condition is that the costume should be appropriate to the subject and, if the personages be historical, one should keep as far as possible to the costume of the period. That of ancient Romans is the most dignified of all, and there is not one that allows the leg more freedom' (Quoted by Beaumont in *Five Centuries of Ballet Design.)*

Le Pavillon d'Armide

Ballet in one act and three scenes by
Alexandre Benois
Composer: Nicolas Tcherepnine
Conductor: Nicolas Tcherepnine
Choreographer: Michel Fokine
Designer: Alexandre Benois
Principals:
Armida: Anna Pavlova
Viscount: Pavel Gerdt
Armida's slave: Vaslav Nijinsky
Mariinsky Theatre, St Petersburg,
25 November 1907

10

Alexandre Benois

(1870–1960)

Costume design for two of King
Hydraot's courtiers
Pencil, indian ink and watercolour
Signed in ink Alexandre Benois
Inscribed '*Le Pavillon d'Armide*
Personnages de la cour du Roi
Hydraot', and erased pencil
inscription
313 × 240
(S.30–1976)

Provenance
Sotheby's, London
Purchased with funds given by
Sir Max (now Lord) Rayne

Exhibition
London, The Leicester Galleries, *The
Dance*, June–July 1938, no. 41

Scene two with the title *The Animated Tapestry* had been performed at the Mariinsky Theatre on 15 April 1907. The whole ballet was revived by Diaghilev's Ballets Russes at the Théâtre du Châtelet, Paris, on 18 May 1909.

Vaudeville Vanities

Revue in three parts by Archibald
de Bear
Part two *A Venetian Wedding* by
Louis N. Parker
Composer: H. Fraser-Simson
Choreographer: Herbert Mason
Designer: Laurence Irving
Principals:
Scaramouche/Leandro:
J. H. Roberts
Pantaleone: Harry Winton
Arlecchino: Basil Howes
Colombina: Mimi Crawford
Vaudeville Theatre, 16 November
1926

11

Laurence Irving

(1897–1988)

Costume design for J. H. Roberts as
Leandro in *A Venetian Wedding*
Pencil and watercolour
Signed with monogram
400 × 285
(S.26–1982)

Provenance
The Fine Art Society
Mark Lynn

Exhibition
London, The Fine Art Society, May
1927, no. 61

Literature
The Independent, London,
27 October 1988, ill.

'. . . an additional asset in Mr. Laurence Irving, a member of the famous theatrical family, who has designed many of the dresses and scenes. Mr. Irving's work is admirable, and, if it were for this alone, the *revue* would be in a class by itself . . . Mr. Irving's work is at its best in the best part of the entertainment, the *ballet* called *A Venetian Wedding*, which forms the whole of the middle part . . . Mr. Irving provides an attractive background and charming dresses.'
The Times, 18 November 1926

'Mr. Irving's costumes here are very good indeed, and should be sufficient in themselves to secure the success of any revue.'
Unidentified press cutting

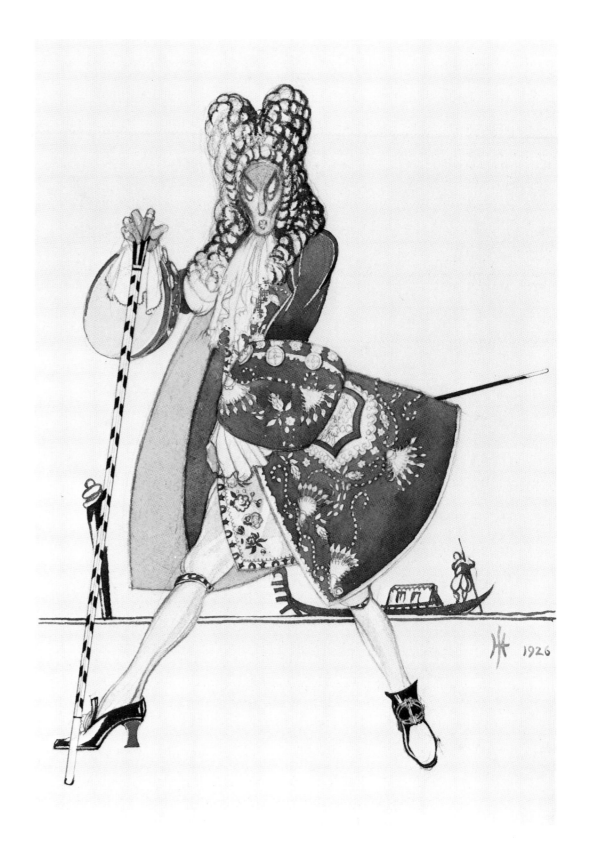

Venice Preserv'd or *A Plot Discovered*

Tragedy in five acts by
Thomas Otway
Director: Peter Gill
Designer: Alison Chitty
Composer: Dominic Muldowney
Principals:
Priuli: Brewster Mason
Jaffier: Michael Pennington
Pierre: Ian McKellen
Belvidera: Jane Lapotaire
Antonio: Hugh Paddick
National Theatre (Lyttelton),
12 April 1984

12
Alison Chitty

(born 1948)

Costume designs for

a   Ian McKellen as Pierre

b   Jane Lapotaire as Belvidera

Pencil and watercolour, with
swatches attached
Inscribed 'Pierre. Ian McKellen',
'Belvidera: Jane Lapotaire, 2 the
same'
375 × 275
(S.1407/1408–1986)

Provenance
Given by the artist

Exhibition
London, Victoria and Albert
Museum, *130 set and costume
designs from the Theatre Museum*,
10 September 1985–27 April 1986

Cendrillon

Ballet in three parts after Perrault's
fairy tale
Composer: Frederic d'Erlanger
Choreographer: Michel Fokine
Designer: Natalia Gontcharova
Principals:
Cinderella: Tatiana Riabouchinska
The Prince: David Lichine
Royal Opera House, Covent Garden,
19 July 1938

13

Natalia Gontcharova

(1881–1962)

Costume design for David Lichine as
the Prince, and for two Ladies of the
Court
Pencil and watercolour
Signed N. G.
380 × 530
(S.519–1980)

Provenance
John Carr Doughty

'It was a happy idea to rescue the story from the conventional eighteenth-century setting,
and the designer is in her happiest mood amid medieval pomps and heraldic splendours.
The settings and drop curtains and, with one or two exceptions, the costumes are a continual delight to the eye. The whole conception shows a quite unusual sense of theatre.'
The Times, 20 July 1938

'The costumes, avoiding powder-and-patch prettiness, follow a sturdier convention,
Perrault, not chocolate-box, in style.'
The Observer, 24 July 1938

Gloriana

Opera in three acts by
Benjamin Britten
Libretto by William Plomer based
on Lytton Strachey's book *Elizabeth
and Essex* (1928)
Conductor: John Pritchard
Director: Basil Coleman
Choreographer: John Cranko
Designer: John Piper
Principals:
Queen Elizabeth I: Joan Cross
Robert Devereux, Earl of Essex:
Peter Pears
Royal Opera House, Covent Garden,
8 June 1953

14

John Piper

(born 1903)

Costume design for Joan Cross as
Queen Elizabeth I
Pencil, ink and watercolour with
swatches attached 'red lining of
taffetas', 'stock', 'stock'
Signed in ink John Piper
Inscribed 'Act II sc.1 Q.E.',
'Gloriana, The Queen, Act II sc 1.
(second costume)', 'medallions',
'cotton N.B.'
567 × 387
(S.1763–1986)

Provenance
Given by the artist

'Tradesmen and flower-arrangers worked late into last night at the Royal Opera House, preparing for Covent Garden's most brilliant occasion. Tonight the Queen and the Duke of Edinburgh, most of the Royal Family, the Cabinet, leaders of the Opposition, visiting foreign dignitaries, and 1,500 members of the public go there for the Royal Gala Première of Benjamin Britten's Coronation opera "Gloriana".'
Daily Mail, 8 June 1953

'John Piper's scenery and costumes were some of the most beautiful any of us have seen. He completely avoided Ye Olde Englishe, and dreamed up a wondrous, fantastic world of softly fused yet rich colours and timeless Greek-Tudor-rococo-Victorian-modern architecture.'
Cecil Smith, *Daily Express*, 9 June 1953

'John Piper . . . has here greatly enlarged his range and included several radiantly bright scenes, and his costumes mingle in their hundreds to ring subtle changes of colour harmony. None but the very youngest of us, we all fondly hope, will ever see a Coronation again, and none may ever witness anything so gorgeous at Covent Garden.'
Eric Blom, *The Observer*, 14 June 1953

"King Lear"
Laurence Olivier
first costume
I

King Lear
by William Shakespeare
Director: Laurence Olivier
Designer: Roger Furse
Composer: Alan Rawsthorne
Principals:
King Lear: Laurence Olivier
Earl of Kent: Nicholas Hannen
Earl of Gloucester: George Relph
Fool: Alec Guinness
Goneril: Pamela Brown
Regan: Margaret Leighton
Cordelia: Joyce Redman
Old Vic Company
New Theatre (now Albery),
24 September 1946

15
Roger Furse

(1903–72)

Costume design for Laurence Olivier
as King Lear in scene 1
Pencil, crayon and watercolour,
with swatches
Signed in pencil R Furse
Inscribed '"King Lear"/Laurence
Olivier/First costume', '$28\frac{1}{2} \times 19\frac{1}{2}$'
585×388
(Circ.61–1954)

Provenance
Given by the artist
Circulation Department, Victoria
and Albert Museum

Exhibition
London, Victoria and Albert
Museum, *Modern British Stage
Design*, November 1951–January
1952, no. 30 (subsequently on tour)

Literature
Brown, Ivor, *The Masque*, no. 1
December 1946, ill. p. 6

Realism and reality

This group of designs, subdivided into smaller sections, aims to show how designers have tried in different ways to create a sense of real life on the stage behind the rigid and often incongruously ornate proscenium arch.

One of the most influential companies in the latter half of the nineteenth century was the Meiningen Court Theatre of the Duchy of Saxe-Meiningen in Germany. The enterprise was directed by three people of exceptional talent with fertile and original ideas about the art of theatre. The triumvirate consisted of the Duke himself, Georg II, who was an accomplished artist and drew many of the production sketches with great verve, his third wife, the actress Ellen Franz, and his stage director Ludwig Chronegk. Between 1874–90 the company gave 2,591 performances touring most of the major European cities including Berlin, Vienna, Budapest, Moscow, St Petersburg, Copenhagen, Stockholm, Amsterdam, Brussels and London. The Duke established the essential principle of relating the stage picture to the actor as naturally as possible. As Lee Simonson in *The Stage is Set* has observed: 'Every tradition of routine repertory based on opera was discredited and a method of bringing plays to life on the boards was everywhere recognized as nothing less than a new art.'

Designers know that reality is not the same as realism.

Diagonal perspective

The invention, by the Bibienas, of a setting placed at an angle of forty-five degrees (*scena per angolo*) so that it ran diagonally off the stage created a much larger sense of space. It also gave everyone in the auditorium a more acceptable view than with strict symmetrical settings and put nearly every member of the audience on equal terms.

Baroque architectural settings were often, and sometimes still are, built in perspective so that the actor is only in scale when down stage. Now, since the actor generally uses the whole stage, designers (for example Reece Pemberton [No. 17]) let the natural perspective take its effect on the eye of the spectator.

The Duke of Saxe-Meiningen also rejected symmetry because it was unnatural. His principles of stagecraft were described in a document first published in 1909. This document begins: 'In the composition of the set care must be taken to ensure that its centre is not identical with the centre of the stage. If the composition is organised around the geometrical centre two equal halves will be produced, and then there is always the danger that in the disposition of the groups and their incorporation in the whole a more or less symmetrical balance between right and left will be created, which will be wooden, inflexible, and uninteresting in its effect'. (Paul Lindau, 'Herzog Georg von Meiningen als Regisseur' in *Die Deutsche Bühne* quoted by John Osborne (see bibliography).)

16
Ferdinando Galli da Bibiena

(1657–1743)

Design for an unknown setting
Pen and ink, and wash
235 × 368
(f.56–3)

Provenance
Harry R. Beard Theatre Collection
Given by the executors of
Harry R. Beard

Literature
Rogers, Jean Scott, *Stage by Stage*,
(London, 1985), ill. no. 23, p. 40

Waters of the Moon

Comedy in three acts by
N. C. Hunter
Director: Frith Banbury
Designers: Reece Pemberton (sets);
Gladys Cobb (costumes)
Principals:
Evelyn Daly: Wendy Hiller
Mrs Whyte: Sybil Thorndike
Colonel Selby: Harold Scott
Mrs Ashworth: Kathleen Harrison
Helen Lancaster: Edith Evans
Theatre Royal, Haymarket,
19 April 1951

17

Reece Pemberton

(1914–77)

Set designs

a for Act I and Act II scene 2: The
lounge of an hotel on the edge of
Dartmoor
100 × 160
(S.472–1987)

b for Act II scene 1 and Act III:
The garden
100 × 155
(S.471–1987)

c another version for the garden
98 × 154
(S.469–1987)

d another version for the garden
98 × 144
(S.470–1987)

Each pencil, pen and ink and
watercolour

Provenance
The artist
Given by Mrs Reece Pemberton

'In ancient days there used to be a play called "The Rival Queens", in which London used to delight to watch the great ladies of the playhouse trying to act one another off the boards. . . . To-day, stage methods are gentler. But still, those who go to the Haymarket to see N. C. Hunter's "Waters of the Moon" will capture something of the old-time thrill as they watch Dame Sybil Thorndike and Dame Edith Evans share the honours of a finely acted play.'
W. A. Darlington, *The Daily Telegraph*, 26 April 1951

Only one critic mentioned the designer.

'Reece Pemberton's settings are the very essence of Devon gloom, snow and sunlight.'
The Stage, 3 May 1951

The reality must have been totally successful.

Romantic realism
'The romantic has a particular appeal to the English temperament, nurtured not on the sunshine and clear skies of the south but on mists and nuances of light, creating an atmosphere of mystery. De Loutherbourg conceived his settings as pictures rather than as formal architecture; his perspectives were no longer the formal ones of the Italian style but were broken up in a more natural fashion.'
Sybil Rosenfeld, *A Short History of Scene Design in Great Britain*

Richard III

by William Shakespeare
adapted by Colley Cibber
Designer: Philippe Jacques de Loutherbourg
Richard III: David Garrick
possibly at Theatre Royal, Drury Lane, London, 30 May 1772

18
Philippe Jacques de Loutherbourg

(1740–1812)

Set designs for Act V scene 2
All pen and ink and wash on paper, cut out and laid down on card mount
All signed on mount with monogram (?) CR, dated July 1874

a   landscape with stone bridge in middle distance
Inscribed on mount 'Original sketches made for "Richard the 3rd" by de Loutherbourg for Mr Garrick. The first practical bridge. Presented to H. Irving Esq by his old friend'

b   landscape with baggage train in foreground
Inscribed on mount 'Sketch for the play "Richard the 3rd" made for David Garrick by de Loutherbourg. Presented to H. Irving Esq by his old friend'

c   landscape with tents in middle distance
Inscribed on mount 'The original sketch by de Loutherbourg made for Mr Garrick. Ricard (*sic*) the 3rd. The first practical bridge. Presented to H. Irving Esq by his old friend'

Each 230 × 310 including mount (S.1471/3–1986)

Provenance
? Charles Reade
Sir Henry Irving
Bertram Forsyth
Mrs J Forsyth

Literature
Lawrence, W. J., 'The Pioneers of Modern English Stage-Mounting: Phillipe (*sic*) Jacques de Loutherbourg, R.A.', *The Magazine of Art*, (London, 1895), pp. 172–7, ill. (a) p. 175, (b) p. 177, (c) p. 176
Rosenfeld, Sybil, *Theatre Notebook*, vol. xix, (London, 1964–5), pp. 110–11
Merchant, Moelwyn, *Shakespeare and the Artist*, (London, 1959), pp. 60–4

These collage sketches, reproduced in *The Magazine of Art*, had disappeared until a few years ago when the Theatre Museum acquired them. The three sketches are made of small drawings cut out and pasted on to a plain background. Dr. Richard Southern, working from the photographs in *The Magazine of Art*, thought these fragments had been assembled wrongly and reconstructed them into two scenes – one 'a rocky country with a repaired bridge in the middle distance' and the other 'a camp scene with the skycloth missing.' Drawings of his reconstructions are reproduced in *Shakespeare and the Artist* (see Literature above), but further research is needed on these fragmentary sketches.

David Garrick saw that de Loutherbourg 'had the sum-total of Continental scenic resources in his ken' and employed him as his designer at Drury Lane. The innovations he brought to the theatre were the introduction of built pieces of scenery such as the bridge shown here and new methods of lighting the set with border battens so that the whole stage was lit, which meant that the actor was not forced to perform down stage in order to be seen. He also invented machines for making sound effects such as the crack of thunder, the boom of cannon and the lapping of waves. As a result he was the first to bring a kind of naturalism into the theatre.

Original Sketch made for "Richard the 3rd" by De Loutherbourg for Mr Garrick — The first practical Bridge on our old scenes R July 1874

Sketch for the play "Richard the 3rd" – Made for David Garrick by De Loutherbourg –

Presented to Henry Irving Esq by his old friend CF July 1874

The original sketch by de Loutherbourg made for Mr Garrick — Richard the 3.d — The first practical bridge

Presented to Henry Irving Esq. by his old friend [monogram] July. 1874.

Richard III
by William Shakespeare
Unidentified production

19

Thomas Grieve
(1799–1882)

Design for a set
Watercolour laid on card
Inscribed on card 'Richard III',
'Thomas Grieve'
154 × 227
(S.1015–1984)

Provenance
The family of the artist

'The painted perspective still has a great future, for far greater variety can be got out of paint and canvas than out of any three dimensional arrangement of cubes, scenes and lights.'

George W. Harris

(This quotation and the one after No. 22 are from a lecture given to the Liverpool Medical and Literary Society and reprinted in the catalogue of the exhibition *George W. Harris* at the Walker Art Gallery, Liverpool, 26 April–18 May 1958.)

The Grieves were a family of scene painters who worked for many London theatres during the greater part of the nineteenth century. The father, John Henderson (1770–1845), was principally connected with Covent Garden. His two sons, Thomas and William (1800–44), also started at Covent Garden but then worked for other managements. Thomas was later assisted by his son Thomas Walford (1841–?). They developed the art of scene painting which with them evolved from the romantic to the realistic, although they always retained a true, if conventional, sense of theatre.

The production for which this is a design has not been identified. It could possibly be for Charles Kean at the Princess's Theatre in the 1850s.

Giselle

Ballet in two acts by Jules Henri
Vernoy de Saint-Georges and
Théophile Gautier based on a theme
of Heinrich Heine
Composer: Adolphe Adam
Conductor: Constant Lambert
Choreographer: Nicholas Sergeyev
after Jean Coralli
Designer: James Bailey
Principals:
Giselle: Margot Fonteyn
Count Albrecht: Alexis Rassine
The Sadler's Wells Ballet Company
Royal Opera House, Covent Garden,
12 June 1946

20

James Bailey

(1922–1980)

Set design for act 1: Giselle's cottage
in the wood
Pencil, pen and ink and watercolour
Signed in ink James Bailey
Inscribed 'Sketch for Giselle Act I
Sadler's Wells Ballet Covent
Garden'
320 × 460
(S.1581(225)–1984)

Provenance
Given by the beneficiaries of the
artist's estate

Literature
Bailey, James, 'Designing the
Classical Ballet', *Souvenirs de Ballet*,
no. 1, (London, 1949), pp. 90–2

'In designing the production for Covent Garden I endeavoured to create a setting which would be as acceptable to a modern audience as it would have been to one in the nineteenth century which saw the original *Giselle* . . . I felt that the only way to present this Ballet was to dress it and set it completely in the convention of the last century. To give it a romantic setting on a large scale, no half-measures, no modern ideas creeping in, no doing it in sepias and greys . . . I set out to make the first act the naturalistic charming woodland scene I thought it should be. Early morning – a backcloth of pale misty mountains of a slightly strange form in the distance – trees, with the leaves cut and netted – Giselle's cottage with imitation thatch, vine leaves and bunches of grapes, which could be picked, pots of geraniums and marguerites, many details which are now considered old-fashioned, but which, if carefully handled can have much appeal.'
James Bailey, *Designing the Classical Ballet*

'From the rise to the fall of the curtain the romantic and tragic atmosphere of this story was both seen and felt by the audience. This was in no small way due to the decor and costumes by James Bailey, who must be congratulated on his complete understanding of the task and his treatment of it.

The first act with its typical North German cottage and barn, its vines and glimpses of the distinctive outlines of the Harz mountains with a castle set among the woods, was a true framework for the realistic side of the ballet.'
The Sitter Out, *The Dancing Times*, July 1946

(See also No. 29.)

Jack and the Beanstalk

Pantomime by Arthur Sturgess and
Arthur Collins
Composer: J. M. Glover
Designers: Bruce Smith, W. Perkins
and McCleary, R. Caney, H. Emden,
W. Cross, W. Harford (sets); Comelli
(costumes)
Principal:
Mrs Kelly (Dame Trot): Dan Leno
Theatre Royal Drury Lane,
26 December 1899

21
Robert Caney

(1847–1911)

Set design for Part I, scene 6:
The roofs of the city
Pencil, pen and ink and watercolour
Signed R.C.
190 × 265
(S.861–1981)

Provenance
Christopher Powney

Exhibition
London, Victoria and Albert
Museum, *Images of Show Business*,
17 November 1982–17 April 1983,
no. 67

Literature
Fowler, James (editor), *Images of
Show Business*, (London, 1982), ill.
no. 67

The magic of the beanstalk works because the rest of the set is as realistic as possible.

Hassan

Play in five acts by James Elroy
Flecker, arranged by Basil Dean
Director: Basil Dean
Composer: Frederick Delius
Choreographer: Michel Fokine
Designer: George W. Harris
Principals:
Hassan: Henry Ainley
Selim: Esmé Percy
Yasmin: Cathleen Nesbitt
The Caliph: Malcolm Keen
Ishak: Leon Quartermaine
His Majesty's Theatre,
20 September 1923

22
George W. Harris
(1878–1929)

Set design for the confectioner's
shop
Pencil and watercolour
Signed in pencil G. W. Harris
228 × 302
(S.1333–1986)

Provenance
Blackwell's, Oxford

'A point must be made in a design as it is in dialogue, not over- or under-stated, and the eye of the observer must be drawn to those features which distinguish or give character to the play he is called upon to decorate.'
George W. Harris (See No. 19)

'The new approach to scene design by way of light called for revolutionary changes in scene-painting techniques as well. The distempered surfaces of the canvas required special treatments to evoke the required light response. Harris employed various novel devices to secure these effects. He was always experimenting with stipples of various colours and textures, and sometimes with the surfaces of the canvas itself. For example, in the *Hassan* street scene he worked ground mica in with the size and distemper, so that in the early morning sun the walls glistened with iridescent effect.'
Basil Dean in foreword to exhibition catalogue *George W. Harris* (Liverpool, 1958)

The drawing-room comedy box

Someone invented the convention of a totally false but completely plausible drawing-room for light comedy plays. The sets usually have three walls and part of a ceiling; there are doors where in a real house no door could possibly be; there are always French windows leading into an invisible garden; there is always a sofa in the middle of the room as well as a table for an over-used telephone; and there is often a staircase to an architecturally impossible upper floor, but down which grand actresses can make impressive entrances.

Private Lives

Comedy in three acts by
Noël Coward
Director: Noël Coward
Designer: Gladys Calthrop
Principals:
Sybil Chase: Adrianne Allen
Elyot Chase: Noël Coward
Victor Prynne: Laurence Olivier
Amanda Prynne:
Gertrude Lawrence
Phoenix Theatre, 24 September
1930

23
Gladys Calthrop

(*c*. 1900–80)

Set design for Act II and III:
Amanda's flat in Paris
Pen and ink, and watercolour
Signed G. L Calthrop
Inscribed 'Private Lives rough sketch scene ii & iii', 'Toile de (?)Trice walls. Wooden curtains and pelmets/painted – also alcove pillars/French empire and modern furniture./black oilsilk (?) curtains. doors painted with pillars & arch./ chair and sofa covered tweed'
361 × 531 overall, 226 × 379 image
(S.475–1989)

Provenance
Given by the executors of Gladys
Calthrop

'The piece, as has been suggested, is brilliantly acted. Mr Laurence Olivier and Miss Adrianne Allen handsomely pretend to absence of brains and breeding. Mr Coward runs the full gamut of grimace, giggle, and gaminerie; in the sumptuous décor he is the exotic baby sprawling upon Aubusson. As for Miss Gertrude Lawrence I will only say that to assess her talent I should assemble as jury Mesdames Tempest and Printemps, Fontanne and Arnaud. For these artists know what is what, and Miss Lawrence answers expectation's every beck and call.'
James Agate, *The Sunday Times*, 28 September 1930

It is strange how many really important moments in life slip by in the procession, unnoted, and devoid of prescience. No guardian angel whacks a sharp triangle in the brain, and the heavens remain commonplace. It is not my intention in this book to delve deeply into personal relationships, but as Gladys Calthrop has been so intimately concerned with all my best work, and so intrinsically part of my failures and successes, I feel that a small, retrospective fanfare is not entirely out of place.'
Noël Coward, *Present Indicative*

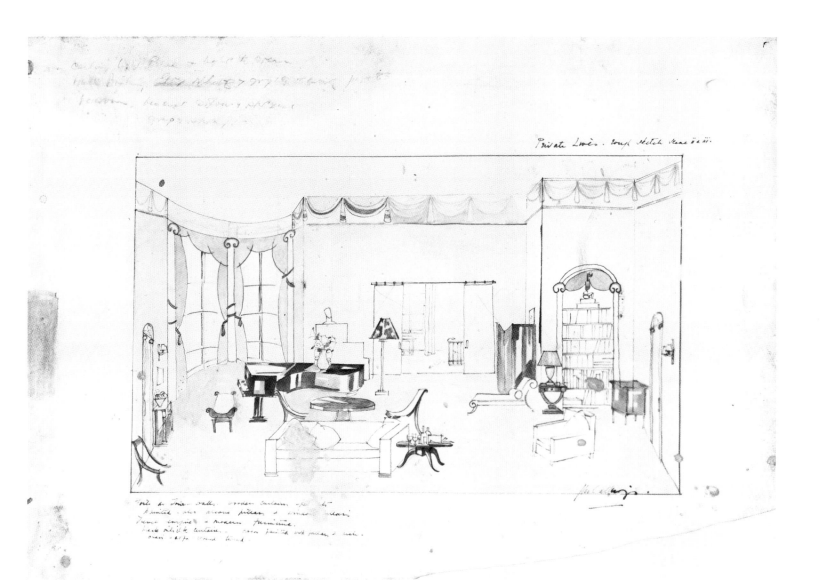

Dear Charles

Comedy in three acts by Alan
Melville after *Les Enfants d'Edouard*
by Marc-Gilbert Sauvajon and
Frederick Jackson
Director: Murray MacDonald
Designer: Hutchinson Scott (set)
Principals:
Denise: Yvonne Arnaud
Jan Letzaresco: Charles Goldner
New Theatre (now Albery),
18 December 1952

24

J. Hutchinson Scott

(1924–77)

Design for the permanent set: the
living room of the Darvels' house in
Paris
Pen and ink, watercolour
heightened with white, mounted on
card
Signed in ink J. Hutchinson Scott
August 1952
Inscribed in ink 'Dear Charles'
Inscribed in pencil 'black carpet
and stair carpet (or dark blue grey)',
'black and white checked stage
cloth or pink and grey? better ?',
'crystal wall fittings for lights bottle
green stain drape', 'black and gold
bannisters', 'French grey walls/
white on frieze etc', 'balcony
supported by metal trellis work
columns (black & gold)', 'pictures in
old gold velvet frames', 'black silk
rope gold bosses handrail', 'painted
flowers', 'unpolished limewood
doors', 'white porcelain door
furniture', 'wood surrounded to
fire', 'wooden mantel supported by
gold cherubs', 'blue and white
tartan type wool', 'bamboo',
'bamboo table before fire', 'cedar
wood frames – books', 'bottle green
velvet on chaise & armchair
unpolished wood', '*Shutters* pink &
white swagged drapes white linen
sun blinds also covers to single
chairs', 'rosewood and unpolished
furniture'
452 × 568
(S.460–1981)

Provenance
Murray MacDonald Bequest

'Not long ago a theatre manager told me that what he wanted critics to say about his
plays was that they would run for ever . . . I think I am speaking the exact truth when
I say that "Dear Charles" at the New, will run for at least a year . . . It is perfectly cast.
Murray MacDonald has produced it with deftness, and Hutchinson Scott has set it in
splendour.'
W. A. Darlington, *The Daily Telegraph*, 19 December 1952

73

The Old Ladies

Play in three acts by Rodney
Ackland adapted from the novel by
Hugh Walpole
Director: Frith Banbury
Designer: Reece Pemberton (set)
Principals:
Lucy Amorest: Mary Jerrold
May Beringer: Jean Cadell
Agatha Payne: Mary Clare
Lyric Theatre, Hammersmith,
4 October 1950

25

Reece Pemberton

(1914–77)

Design for the permanent set: an old
house in Pontippy Square,
Polchester at the turn of the century
Pencil, pen and ink and gouache
361 × 556
(S.1280–1983)

Provenance
The artist
Given by Mrs Reece Pemberton

The play, also with Mary Jerrold and Jean Cadell in the cast, was originally produced at the New (now Albery) Theatre, London on 3 April 1935 directed by John Gielgud.

'Is there still a wide public for stage horrors – the kind of Grand Guignol play designed expressly and cunningly to curdle the audience's blood?
The question was posed (and perhaps answered) at the Lyric Theatre, Hammersmith, last night with the revival, after 15 years of "The Old Ladies". Rodney Ackland's skilful adaptation of the Hugh Walpole novel – just three characters in a composite setting of three bed-sitting rooms – won the same gasps, nervous giggles and prolonged cheers as of old.'
Harold Conway, *Evening Standard*, 5 October 1950

'Frith Banbury's revival is slow, but absorbing. He is helped by a clever set showing the three old ladies' bedrooms at once. But I'm glad I left my mother safe at home.'
John Barber, *Daily Express*, 5 October 1950

'The staircase, too, is excellent: out of its shadows and bends, the horrible, bloated Mrs Pyne can emerge with an effect terrifying and loathsome.
   Up and down these stairs, in and out of doors, the serene Mrs Amorest, the frightened and twittering Miss Beringer, and the dreadful Mrs Payne are constantly on the move, and a play that could easily become stale is kept visually alive. All this is much to Mr Pemberton's credit. Had the ingenuity of his design permitted him to provide Miss Beringer's room with a true window, his triumph would have been perfect.'
Harold Hobson, *The Sunday Times*, 8 October 1950

The Skin of Our Teeth

A history of the world in comic
strip in three acts
by Thornton Wilder
Director: Laurence Olivier
Composer: Leslie Bridgewater
Designers: Roger Furse (set); L&H
Nathan, Sally Spruce, Moss Bros.,
and Lily Taylor (costumes)
Principals:
Sabina: Vivien Leigh
Mrs Antrobus: Joan Young
Mr Antrobus: Cecil Parker
Fortune-teller: Ena Burrill
Phoenix Theatre, 16 May 1945

26

Roger Furse

(1903–72)

Design for the set
Pencil and gouache
Signed R. Furse
329 × 386 overall, 262 × 381 image
(Circ.60–1954)

Provenance
Association of Theatrical Designers
and Craftsmen
Given by the artist
Circulation Department, Victoria
and Albert Museum

Exhibition
London, Victoria and Albert
Museum, *Modern British Stage
Design*, November 1951–January
1952, no. 28 (subsequently on tour)

'A silly, a wise, a diverting play. Mr Wilder has set out to write a stage history of mankind
in terms of the comic strip. That is to say, he devotes several pictures to every statement,
however simple. The actors move capriciously in and out of the stage framework,
soliloquizing to their hearts' content, complaining to the stage manager that this or that
scene is hardly worth playing, revelling in anachronisms and speaking sometimes as representative figures. The author's first problem is to use the unfamiliar technique with
such precision that he makes what he has to say perfectly plain and highly diverting.
In this perilous task he succeeds handsomely.'
The Times, 17 May 1945

'Like the real world, the world of the theatre has grown fantastic, and every first class designer takes this into account. Drama is launched upon a visionary career and design has become allegorical. Except in the boulevard theatre and in drawing-room comedy we no longer find realistic interiors enclosed between three walls, with the audience in the place of the fourth. Remoter planes are indicated at the back of the set, perspective and projected scenery are often used and "transformation scenes" predominate. The imaginary world of dramatic events has taken on the value of a symbol, the contours of the playing space remain in view and its own particular reality supplants the imitation of real life. Thanks to true proportions and dimensions consciously revealed, the stage has been recovered for the actor.'
Ingvelde Muller, 'Theatre Design in Germany', *World Theatre*, vol. iii no. 3, 1954

Plain and fancy dress

For costumes in realistic plays the designer has to achieve a nice balance between realism – the actor's own clothes, and theatricality – costume that fits the character, combines with the ensemble and still looks convincing under spotlights from the gallery or the back of the stalls.

The only limit to the designer's imagination when he thinks of costumes for pantomime and revue is a practical one: can the costume be made and can it be worn?

—

'The costume of the actor is the heightening, the translation into theatrical terms, of the dress of everyday life. It is the selection from the vast store of actual material, of what is suitable, beautiful and helpful to the portrayal of character. When this is skilfully done the artist is not merely the copyist of a period, even if it is the style of our own time, but he is a real creator; and this principle applies to all costume designed for the stage, whether for the straight drama, comedy, tragedy or the more fantastic forms of ballet, vaudeville and musical extravaganza.'
Aline Bernstein, 'The Costume Museum', *Theatre Arts Monthly*, October 1937

This section is subdivided into two groups to show the difference in approach between realism and fantasy.

Everyday and workaday costume

'What he tried to do, and what he succeeded in doing, was to think, himself, in terms of the chosen period, to design his dresses as if he were indeed himself a contemporary of the people in the play to be decorated, and not as if he were a modern painter reconstructing a bygone era. He held that only thus could a living and truly dramatic thing be created out of the past, and he wished his work to be as distinct as possible from a mere piece of museum reconstruction, which he always thought utterly unsuitable to the needs of a theatre.'
Nigel Playfair on Claud Lovat Fraser, 'Costume at the Lyric Theatre Hammersmith', in G. Sheringham and M. Morrison *Robes of Thespis*

What Nigel Playfair describes is not unique to Claud Lovat Fraser but is what every designer of costume tries to do.

27
Studio of Daniel Rabel

(active 1613–34)

Costume design for M. Ferrant as a pastry cook in an unknown ballet
Pen and ink, watercolour
Inscribed 'Ferrant', 'paticier', 'Coiffure d'un pasté', 'manche de taffetas bleu, froussiré', 'forme de tartelette faite de claye ou de pasté', 'taffetas blanc', 'de mesme, coiffé d'un pasté', numbered '159'
324 × 211
(S.1147–1986)

Provenance
Sotheby's, London
Purchased with assistance from the National Art-Collections Fund

Exhibition
London, Theatre Museum, *The King's Pleasures – newly discovered designs for the Court Ballet of Louis XIII*, 24 April–2 August 1987

Literature
McGowan, Margaret M., *The Court Ballet of Louis XIII*, (London, 1987), ill. no. 175

The character of a pastry cook appeared in both the *Ballet du Landy* (1627), and the *Ballet de la Debauche* (c. 1633)

ferrant

159.

patiiir

Coiffure d'un pas

mouche d bibete
houstine

forme
tartelette
la Plare
du paste

taffetas blan

de mesme, Coiffé d'un pasté

81

Cavaliers and Roundheads

Operatic drama by Isaac Pocock
adapted from *Old Mortality* by
Walter Scott and music from
'popular Scotch airs' and Bellini's
I Puritani
Principals:
Colonel Grahame of Claverhouse:
Mr Diddear
Lord Evandale: Mr King
Major Allan: Mr Baker
John Balfour of Burley:
Mr Vandenhoff
Theatre Royal, Drury Lane,
13 October 1835

28

Clarkson Stanfield RA

(1794–1867)

Costume design for John Cooper as
Henry Morton of Milnwood
Watercolour
Inscribed 'This is something (like)
the cut of Harry Morton. Over'
Inscribed on reverse 'If any other
Color but Green, a bright buff, to
match belt and boots. – the Color of
the feather may be red or black –
black best perhaps unless there is
any red binding on the dress, which
must be generally Green.
This sketch is barbarious, but I
work by night and on paper that
will not take Color properly. It will
however be sufficient to shew what
is wanted.'
227 × 186
(GEP.11–1953)

Provenance
Gabrielle Enthoven Collection

The period is supposed to be the seventeenth century during the Civil War in England
between the supporters of the King and Cromwell.

This is something the cut of Henry Martin.

Giselle

(See No. 20 for production details)

29

James Bailey

(1922–80)

Costume design for two huntsmen
in Act I
Pen and ink and watercolour
Signed James Bailey
Inscribed 'Design for 2 Huntsmen/
act I Giselle'
340 × 254
(S.1581 (227)–1984)

Provenance
Given by the beneficiaries of the
artist's estate

No huntsman ever wore a costume like this, but this is a costume for a dancer. The designer, however, has successfully achieved the feeling of reality while keeping to the convention of a male dancer's costume being composed of tight trousers and a short jacket.

design for
2 Hauptmen

act I. Snelle.

Ernest Gardog

The Beggar's Opera

Opera in three acts by John Gay
Composer: John Christopher
Pepusch
New settings and additional music:
Frederic Austin
Conductor: Eugene Goossens
Director: Nigel Playfair
Designer: Claud Lovat Fraser
Principals:
Peachum: Frederic Austin
Lockit: Arthur Wynn
Macheath: Frederick Ranalow
Polly Peachum: Sylvia Nelis
Lyric Theatre, Hammersmith,
5 June 1920

30
Claud Lovat Fraser

(1890–1921)

Costume design for Arthur Wynn as
Lockit
Pen, ink and watercolour
Signed C. Lovat Fraser, dated 1920
Inscribed 'Lockit (Arthur Wynn)'
191 × 106
(Circ.312–1928)

Provenance
Freda O'Leary
Circulation Department, Victoria
and Albert Museum

A note in the programme stated: 'In this version of Mr Gay's famous *English Ballad Opera* every possible effort has been made to recapture the spirit of the original work, much of which was 'improved away' in the representations of the early nineteenth century.'

The first production was at Lincoln's Inn Fields on 29 January 1728.

LOCKIT.
(ARTHUR WYNNE).

War and Peace

Opera in five acts and thirteen
scenes by Serge Prokofiev and Mira
Mendelson based on the novel by
Leo Tolstoy
Composer: Serge Prokofiev
Project for Metropolitan Opera
House, New York, 1947

31

Mstislav Dobujinsky

(1875–1957)

Costume design for General
Kutuzov
Pencil and watercolour
Signed with monogram MD,
'obujinsky' and '1947 N.Y.' added
later
Inscribed 'W&P', 'Kutusov VII',
'35'
376 × 255
(S.68–1987)

Provenance
Gabrielle Enthoven Collection

This is a wonderful example of a costume design where the painter has also made a character study of General Kutuzov in Prokofiev's opera rather than just drawing a general's uniform.

*HMS Pinafore, or The Lass
that loved a Sailor*

Opera in one act
Composer: Arthur Sullivan
Librettist: W. S. Gilbert
Conductor: Malcolm Sargent
Director: Rupert D'Oyly Carte
Designer: George Sheringham
Principals:
Sir Joseph Porter: Henry A. Lytton
Captain Corcoran: Leo Sheffield
Ralph Rackstraw: Derek Oldham
Josephine: Winnie Melville
Savoy Theatre, 9 December 1929

32

George Sheringham

(1884–1937)

Costume design for Bertha Lewis as
Little Buttercup
Watercolour
343 × 240
(Circ.55–1938)

Provenance
The artist
Mrs George Sheringham
Circulation Department, Victoria
and Albert Museum

An almost exact copy of this design by George Sheringham was in the collection of the
D'Oyly Carte Company until it was given to the Theatre Museum by Dame Bridget D'Oyly
Carte (see also Nos 70–76)

The difference of opinion:
'. . . we must deplore the highly-coloured, fanciful costumes that Mr George Sheringham
has devised for the present production. The period (about 1830) is quite wrong.'
The Times, 10 December 1929

'Mr Sheringham's newly-designed costumes, I did not care for, however. The colours are
too garish and they are not in the period. What about that reference to the telephone?'
P. P. in unidentified newspaper, 10 December 1929

'. . . Mr Sheringham's ingeniously varied reds, whites, and blues, might well have been
as symbolical as the ensign fluttering at the masthead on the good ship Pinafore. But,
symbolical or not, they are enchantingly early-Victorian, and as pretty as any peach.'
E. K., *Daily Telegraph*, 10 December 1929

Petrushka

Ballet in four scenes by Igor
Stravinsky and Alexandre Benois
Composer: Igor Stravinsky
Conductor: Pierre Monteux
Choreographer: Michel Fokine
Designer: Alexandre Benois
Principals:
Petrushka: Vaslav Nijinsky
The Ballerina: Tamara Karsavina
The Moor: Alexandre Orlov
The Showman: Enrico Cecchetti
Diaghilev's Ballets Russes
Théâtre du Châtelet, Paris, 13 June
1911

33
Alexandre Benois

(1870–1960)

Costume design for woman and
child in the crowd
Pencil, watercolour, silver and gold
paint
Signed in Russian Alexandre
Benois, dated 1911
330 × 240
(S.554–1978)

Provenance
Given by Nadia Nerina through the
Friends of the Museum of
Performing Arts

Because this design is signed in Russian, it was almost certainly made for the original
production. (See No. 54.)

The ballet takes places in Admiralty Square, St Petersburg during the Shrovetide Fair
in 1830.

The Cherry Orchard

Play in four acts by Anton Chekhov
Director: Peter Hall
Designer: John Bury
Lighting: David Hersey
Composers: Harrison Birtwistle and
Dominic Muldowney
Choreographer: Sally Gilpin
Principals:
Lopakhin: Albert Finney
Firs: Ralph Richardson
Ranyevskaya: Dorothy Tutin
Gayev: Robert Stephens
National Theatre (Olivier),
14 February 1978

34

John Bury

(born 1925)

Costume design for Albert Finney as
Lopakhin
Pencil and crayon
Signed in pencil John Bury
Inscribed in pencil 'N.T. 1978',
'Albert Finney, Lopakin' (sic)
500 × 315
(S.35–1982)

Provenance
The artist
Riverside Studios

'If I had to pin down the pivotal performance in this production, however, it would be Albert Finney's superb Lopakhin. Again there is the same double vision: he sees himself as a pragmatic businessman whereas he is really governed by love of Ranevskaya and the vanity of the self-made . . . his Lopakhin is squat, barrel-chested, an ambulatory toby-jug with a fob-watch.'
Michael Billington, *The Guardian*, 15 February 1978

This drawing shows that there was obviously a close rapport between designer, director and actor.

ALBERT FINNEY

LOPAKIN

N.T 1978

IV

R Schwabe

S.194-1982

Romeo and Juliet
by William Shakespeare
Director: Basil Sydney assisted by
Edith Craig
Designers: John Bull (sets),
Randolph Schwabe (costumes)
Principals:
Romeo: Basil Sydney
Mercutio: Leon Quartermaine
Juliet: Doris Keane
Nurse to Juliet: Ellen Terry
Lyric Theatre, 12 April 1919

35
Randolph Schwabe

(1885–1948)

Costume design for Doris Keane as
Juliet in Act IV
Charcoal and watercolour
Signed R. Schwabe
Inscribed 'IV' (indicating act 4)
473 × 280
(S.1134–1982)

Provenance
Sir Harry Barnes
The Fine Art Society

Literature
Anon, 'Of "Keane" interest:
"Romeo and Juliet" – costumes' in
The Sketch, London, 9 April 1919,
p. 43: four other costume designs
illustrated

I have included this drawing in this section because the 'historical' effect has been deliberately underplayed producing what is essentially a naturalistic costume.

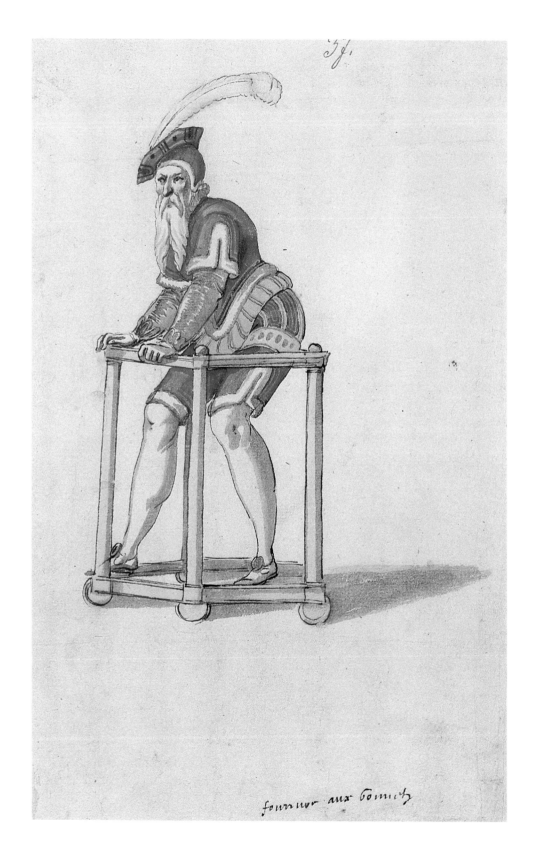

fourneur aux bonnetz

Ballet du Sérieux et du Grotesque

Text by René Bordier
Composer: Antoine Boësset
Louvre, Paris, February 1627

36

Studio of Daniel Rabel

(active 1613–34)

Costume design for an old man
Pen and ink, watercolour
Inscribed 'fourrure aux bonnets'
('fur on the bonnets'), numbered
'37'
290 × 180
(S.1157–1986)

Provenance
Sotheby's, London
Purchased with assistance from the
National Art-Collections Fund

Exhibitions
London, Theatre Museum, *The
King's Pleasures – newly discovered
designs for the Court Ballet of Louis
XIII*, 24 April–2 August 1987

Literature
McGowan, Margaret M., *The Court
Ballet of Louis XIII*, (London, 1987),
ill. no. 107

An almost identical drawing is reproduced as no. 108 in Margaret McGowan's book. This includes an inscription which shows that the part was played by the King's brother and four others.

Fantastical and fanciful

'Costume can express the meaning, the mentality, and the dramatic significance of a given character. If desired, costume can heighten these or reduce them to a symbolical or abstract form. In such ways the costume designer can make manifest the intention of the dramatist. . . . Revue, of course, offers very considerable opportunities for the development of the more spectacular aspects of *mise en scène* . . . Costume for me is one of the most provocative and interesting departments of theatrical experiment.'
Charles B. Cochran, 'Revue' in G. Sheringham and M. Morrison *Robes of Thespis*
But however fantastic the costume may be, the actor must still be convincing whether he is a dog, a dragon or a fairy. Costumes for plays are not the same as costumes for carnivals, pantomimes or floor-shows where it is the spectacular effect that counts above all.

Ballet de la Délivrance de Renaud

by Etienne Durand
Additional verses: R. Bordier
Composers: Pierre Guédron, Gabriel Bataille
Choreographer: Belleville
Designer: Tommaso Francini (sets)
Grande Salle du Louvre, Paris,
29 January 1617

37
Studio of Daniel Rabel

(active 1613–34)

Costume design for character in the form of a dog
Pencil and watercolour
Inscribed in ink 'satin noir chamarré d'argent doublé (?) satin route' (black satin decorated with silver braid lined with red satin') 'peu' ('skin'), 'satin blancq chamarré d'or ('white satin decorated with gold braid') numbered '2' and '64'
285 × 200
(S.1159–1986)

Provenance
Hobhouse Ltd.

Exhibitions
London, Theatre Museum, *The King's Pleasures – newly discovered designs for the Court Ballet of Louis XIII*, 24 April–2 August 1987
Elsinore, Kronborg Castle, *Christian IV and Europe*, 25 March–29 September 1988, no. 543

Literature
McGowan, Margaret M., *The Court Ballet of Louis XIII*, (London, 1987), ill. no. 4

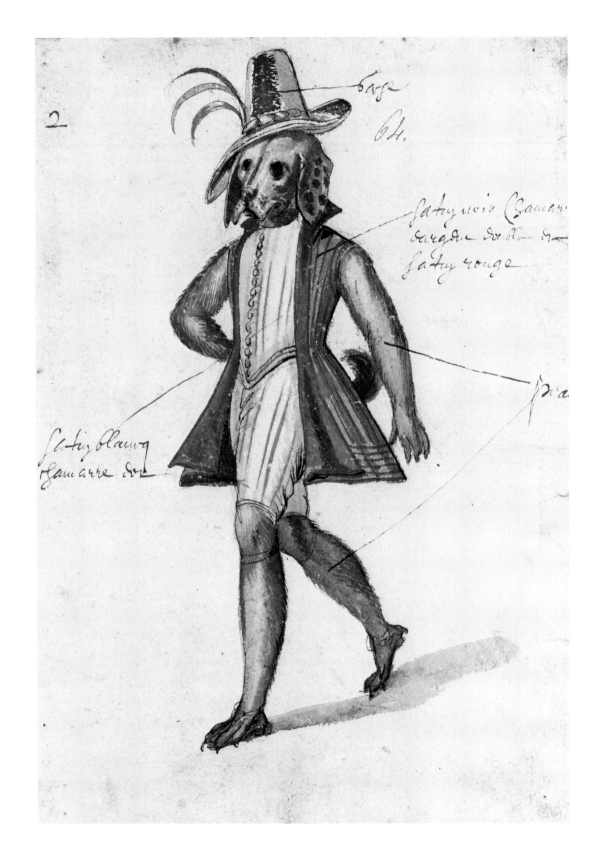

2

bas
64.

satin noir chamar...
dargan doubl... de
satin rouge

satin blancq
chamarre dor

pra...

Where the Rainbow Ends

Play in four acts by Clifford Mills
and John Ramsey
Composer: Roger Quilter
Director: Charles Hawtrey
Designer: Tom Heslewood
Principals:
Rosamund Carey: Esme Wynne
William: Noël Coward
St George of England: Reginald
Owen
The Dragon King: Clifton Anderson
Savoy Theatre, 21 December 1911

38

Tom Heslewood

(1868–1959)

Costume design for Clifton
Anderson as the Dragon King,
second dress
Pencil, watercolour and gouache
Inscribed 'The Dragon King 2nd
dress', 'Dragon King 2nd dress'
375 × 280
(S.280–1982)

Provenance
L. & H. Nathan
Sotheby's, London

'Here it is that George of England comes to the rescue of the children, who have fallen into the hands of the Dragon King, by whom they have been condemned to die. The sword combat that ends in the Dragon King's death is the most thrilling of fights, and leads to the last scene of all, another picture of rare beauty, first dimly seen in purple shadows, and afterwards, when the most real rainbow ever beheld on a stage has faded away, becoming radiant with delicate harmonies of light.'
The Daily Telegraph, 22 December 1911

This critic was totally convinced by the scene.

A Midsummer Night's Dream

by William Shakespeare
Director: Tony Richardson
Designer: Jocelyn Herbert
Principals:
Theseus: Robert Lang
Lysander: Corin Redgrave
Quince: Ronnie Barker
Bottom: Colin Blakely
Flute: Nicol Williamson
Hermia: Rita Tushingham
Helena: Lynn Redgrave
Oberon: Colin Jeavons
Titania: Samantha Eggar
Puck: Alfred Lynch
Royal Court Theatre, 24 January
1962

39

Jocelyn Herbert

(born 1917)

Costume design for one of the fairies
Collage and gouache
300 × 215
(S.2505–1986)

Provenance
Given by the Arts Council of Great
Britain

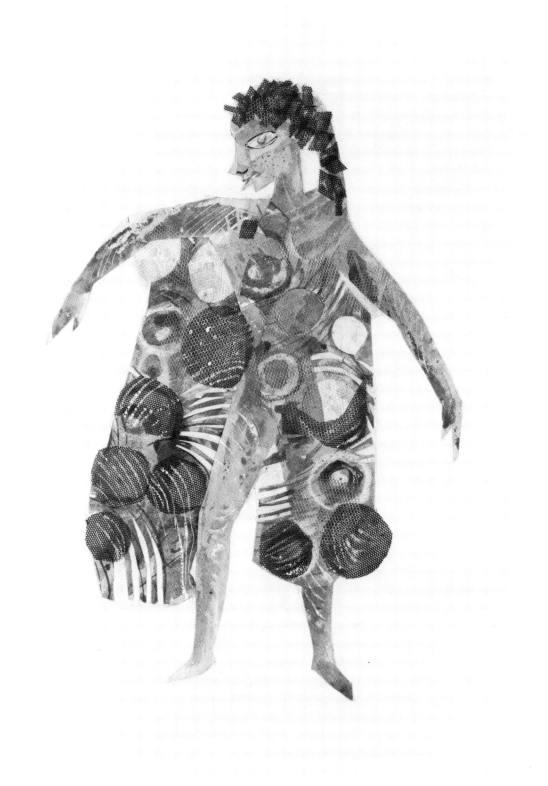

40

Basil Crage

(active 1890s)

Costume designs for unidentified
productions

a one penny postage stamp
Pen and ink and watercolour
222 × 140
(S.752–1983)

b a sunflower
Pencil and watercolour
Signed Basil Crage, dated '95
220 × 120
(S.755–1983)

c a colefish
Pencil and watercolour
Signed Basil Crage, dated '94
214 × 131
(S.761–1983)

Provenance
Mrs C. V. Tinker

These amusing fantasies are probably designs for chorus girls in pantomimes or variety
shows which were popular at the end of the last century.

Colefish.

Babes in the Wood

Pantomime by J. Hickory Wood
and Arthur Collins
Composer: J. M. Glover
Director: Arthur Collins
Designers: R. McCleery, Harry
Brooke, Henry Emden, Bruce Smith,
E. Nichols (sets); Comelli (costumes)
Principals:
Cissie: Marie George
Reggie: Walter Passmore
The Governess: Harry Fragson
Theatre Royal, Drury Lane,
26 December 1907

41

Attilio Comelli

(*c*.1858–1925)

Costume design for six Frozen
Strawberries and six Sugar Sticks in
Part II, scene 7: Lollipop Land
Pencil and watercolour with tinsel
Signed with monogram AC and
dated 1907
Inscribed '6 Frozen Strawberries/
6 Sugar Sticks'
385 × 265
(S.476–1989)

Provenance
Given by George Hoare

The programme only credits Comelli. There were two brothers Comelli, Attilio and E.(?), and although there is some uncertainty about which of them made this design, I think the monogram signature is AC.

110

*L'Orient Merveilleux ou
1002 Nuits de Bagdad*

Ba-Ta-Clan, Paris, 1917

42

Erté (Romain de Tirtoff)

(born 1892)

Costume design for Prince Assad in
Danse du Fouet [*Whip Dance*]
Watercolour, gouache, gold and
silver paint
Signed Erté
Executed March 1917
Inscribed on reverse 'L'Orient
Merveilleux', 'No 18', 'Le Prince
Assad (Danse du Fouet)', 'No 8346'
238 × 150
(Circ.981–1967)

Provenance
Grosvenor Gallery
Circulation Department, Victoria
and Albert Museum

Exhibitions
Travelling exhibition arranged by
the Circulation Department,
Victoria and Albert Museum, 1968
London, Victoria and Albert
Museum, *Images of Show Business*,
17 November 1982–17 April 1983,
no. 60

Literature
Fowler, James (editor), *Images of
Show Business*, (London, 1982), ill.
no. 60

A masterpiece by the undoubted master of the revue costume.

Femmes en Folie

Revue in fifty tableaux by Maurice
Hermite and Jean Le Seyeux
Producer: Paul Derval
Director: Pierre Fréjol
Composers: Maurice Hermite and
Chantrier, Christiné, Moisès Simon,
Neuville, Chagrin Himmel, Rudd
and Leibovici
Conductor: Maurice Hermite
Choreographers: Marguerite
Froman and Miss Bluebell
Designers: Deshays, Boussard and
Sillard (sets); Brunelleschi, Dany,
Jyarmathy (*sic*), Seltenhammer,
Wittop (costumes)
Principals:
André Randall
Spadaro
Viviane Gosset
Jean Sablon
Les Bluebell's Beautiful Ladies
Folies-Bergère, Paris, 1935–6 season

43

L. Dany

(active 1930s)

Costume design for Mademoiselle
Yvette as Une Américaine in *Défense
de . . .* (sketch by André Randall)
Pencil, watercolour and silver paint
Signed L. Dany
Inscribed '*Une américaine*',
'Frédérique (?) ravi avec elle' [(?)
delighted with her]
475 × 315
(S.790–1981)

Provenance
Given by the Friends of the Theatre
Museum (now Theatre Museum
Association)

The titles of all the shows at the Folies Bergère have to have by tradition thirteen letters
and include the word Folie(s). Latterly, the hyphen between 'Folies' and 'Bergère' has
been dropped.

Une américaine

Frédérison
vivi amu a la

L. Bany

44

Umberto Brunelleschi

(1879–1949)

Costume design for Schéhérazade in
an unidentified production
Pencil and watercolour
Signed Brunelleschi
Inscribed 'Schéhérazade'
480 × 315
(S.619 × 1983)

Provenance
Sotheby's, London

Literature
Rogers, Jean Scott, *Stage by Stage*,
(London, 1985), ill. no. 60, p. 60

Brunelleschi worked at the Folies Bergère in Paris in the early 1930s and this design could
be for one of the revues there.

Whisky

C. Gesmar

Mieux que Nue!

Revue in two acts and thirty scenes by Jacques-Charles
Composers: José Padilla, Charles Laurent, Chantrier, Gavel, Scotto, Maurice Yvain
Choreographers: Gertrude Hoffmann and M. Oyra
Director: Jacques-Charles
Designers: Deshayes and Arnaud, Laverdet, Ronsin, Roger and Durand, Canut (sets); Gesmar, Alec Kzewusky, José de Zamora (costumes)
Principals:
Edmonde Guy
Mlle Baldini
Tom Thyl
Eighteen Gertrude Hoffmann Girls
Moulin Rouge Music-Hall, Paris, 1925

45

Charles Gesmar

(1900–1928)

Costume design for Amanda Daisy as Dewar's white label whisky in scene 12: *Rêve Sec* or *La Cave d'un Milliardaire de la 5e Avenue à New York*
Pencil and watercolour
Signed C. Gesmar
Inscribed 'Whisky'
350 × 260
(S.247–1989)

Provenance
Charles Spencer

Exhibitions
London, Arts Club, *The Art of the Theatre*, 15 June–2 September 1988, no. 67

Gesmar, during his tragically short career, was particularly associated with Mistinguett and designed many of her costumes as well as very striking posters for her shows.

Ballet Royal du Grand bal de la Douairière de Billbahaut (The Dowager of Bilbao)

Devised by René Bordier
Composers: Antoine Boësset, Richard, Auget
Additional verses: César de Grand-Pré, Claude de l'Estoile, Imbert
Choreographer: Marais
Designers: Tommaso Francini (sets), Daniel Rabel (costumes)
Principals:
Louis XIII, Marais, members of the Court
Louvre, and Hôtel de Ville, Paris, February 1626

46

Daniel Rabel

(1578–1637)

Costume design for a headless character
Pencil and watercolour
Inscribed '2 hocricanes'
313 × 198
(S.1166–1986)

Provenance
Hobhouse Ltd.

Exhibitions
London, Theatre Museum, *The King's Pleasures – newly discovered designs for the Court Ballet of Louis XIII*, 24 April–2 August 1987

Literature
De Andia, Béatrice (editor), 4 Siècles de ballet à Paris, (Paris, 1985), p. 25
McGowan, Margaret M., *The Court Ballet of Louis XIII*, (London, 1987), ill. no. 72
Arnold, Janet, book review of above, *Theatre Notebook*, vol. XLII no. 2, 1988
Speaight, George, Notes and queries', *Theatre Notebook*, vol. XLIII no. 1, 1989
Fuhring, Peter, *Design into Art*, (London, 1989), p. 413 similar drawing illustrated.

Plus ça change! Joke characters are as old as theatre. This character, all doublet, appeared with another, all hose. Janet Arnold thinks they may reflect a joke at the King's expense 'as on one occasion when he paid his servants too little, they appeared before him half dressed, claiming that they could not afford to buy a whole suit of clothes.' But George Speaight thinks that would have been intolerable *lèse-majesté*, and that the more likely explanation is that they are based on the 'traditional characters of Somebody and Nobody, which were featured as stock figures of popular satire from medieval times to the last century.'

61.

Innovators

'Despite a production being a collaborative effort, the designer is a very lonely animal.'

Ralph Koltai

The history of the theatre is punctuated by people who have changed its course, but this is not a history of the theatre, nor is it a catalogue of the names of all visionaries and reformers.

This section has four drawings by designers who have made a radical contribution to the art of theatre.

Edward Gordon Craig

Craig was really a 'loner' whose enormous influence on the theatre was more effective through his writings than his productions. Influenced by the Italian renaissance theatre, he invented a system of staging with screens which he used in Moscow for his production of *Hamlet*. But here his work is illustrated by a costume design for that production.

'For instance, do not trouble about the costume books. When in great difficulty refer to one in order to see how little it will help you out of your difficulty, but your best plan is never to let yourself become complicated with these things. Remain clear and fresh. If you study how to draw a figure, how to put on it a jacket, coverings for the legs, covering for the head, and try to vary these coverings in all kinds of interesting, amusing, or beautiful ways, you will get much further than if you feast your eyes and confound your brain with Racinet, Planchet, Hottenroth and the others.'
Edward Gordon Craig, 'The Artists of the Theatre of the Future', *On the Art of the Theatre*

Hamlet
by William Shakespeare
Director: Edward Gordon Craig
with Constantin Stanislavsky
Composer: I. Satz
Designer: Edward Gordon Craig
Principals:
Hamlet: Vasili Kachalov
Ophelia: Olga Gzovska
Gertrude: Olga Knipper
Claudius: Nikolai Massalitinov
Laertes: Richard Boleslavsky
Polonius: Vasili Luzhski
Ghost: Nikolai Znamensky
Moscow Art Theatre, 26 December 1911 (8 January 1912)

47
Edward Gordon Craig
(1872–1966)

Costume drawing for Nikolai Znamensky as the Ghost of Hamlet's father
Crayon
Signed EGC, dated 1910
203 × 96
(S.477–1989)

Provenance
Arnold Rood Collection
Given by Professor Arnold Rood

'Hamlet's personal life ran its course in another atmosphere, informed with mysticism. The very first scene of the play realized that life. Mysterious corners, passages, strange lights, deep shadows, moon rays, court sentries, unfathomable underground sounds at the rise of the curtain, choruses of variegated tonalities becoming one with underground blows, the whistling of the wind, and a strange, far-off cry. Meanwhile from among the gray screens that were the walls of the castle emerged the ghost who wandered in his search for Hamlet. He was hardly noticeable, for his costume was of the same colour as the walls. At times he was altogether unseen, then he appeared again in the halftone of the light of a projector. His long cloak dragged behind him. The cries of the sentries frightened him, and he seemed to fade into the niches of the walls and to disappear.'
Constantin Stanislavsky, *My Life in Art*

Ernst Stern and Max Reinhardt

For Reinhardt theatre meant total theatre, pure theatre, 'un-natural' theatre. He has been called the great eclectic, but that is only because he thought that every production had to be treated in its own individual way. He was a continual experimenter, but one of his basic principles was that colour and décor should always be appropriate to the mood of the particular scene. Stern effectively realized the principle for him.

'Doing a Reinhardt' means a production on a colossal scale. Although he is famous for his productions in circuses, exhibition halls and cathedral squares with thousands of spectators, he would just as happily make a production for a few guests in a private house.

Sumurûn

A wordless-musical play in nine tableaux from *Tales of the Arabian Nights* by Friedrich Freksa
Director: Max Reinhardt
Composer: Victor Hollaender
Choreographer: Grete Wiesenthal
Designer: Ernst Stern
Principal:
Sumurûn: Grete Wiesenthal
Deutsches Theater (Kammerspiele), Berlin, 24 April 1910

48

Ernst Stern

(1876–1954)

Set design for scene four: Nur-al-Din's shop
Pencil and watercolour
Signed in pencil Stern
Inscribed 'Teppichladen Sumûrun'
343 × 454
(S.480–1989)

Provenance
Bequeathed by the artist

'Max Reinhardt . . . was influenced by Craig's curtain scenery and his contrasts of light and shade, and he came nearest of all his contemporaries to that amalgam of the artist and practical man which Craig had envisaged. He was an organiser who could unify ideas he had absorbed from many sources. The productions of Craig and Poel had been seen only by limited audiences when Reinhardt brought the mime play, *Sumurûn*, to the Coliseum in 1911. The theatre had a revolving stage which had been installed in 1904, and for his seven tableaux Reinhardt used it so that the main feature of one section served as a subsidiary for the next, thus avoiding the segmental wedge. The story was set in the East but Ernst Stern, the scene designer, obtained his effects not by the sumptuous mounting of *Sardanapalus* but by simple settings with harmonious colour contrasts. The backgrounds were white, against which were set the colours of rugs, the bright wares of a merchant's shop and the effective silhouette of the towers and minarets of the palace against a deep blue sky. Each scene had a dominant colour . . . For the prologue Reinhardt had a Japanese 'flower path' constructed, down which the actor walked through the audience. *Sumurûn* was a sensation and was influential in establishing here simplified setting and an atmospheric unity.'
Sybil Rosenfeld, *A Short History of Scene Design in Great Britain*

Teppichladen.
Summ...

Alexandra Exter and Alexander Tairov

In 1914 Tairov opened the Moscow Kamerny (Chamber) Theatre with an artistic policy of protest against the naturalistic theatre of Stanislavsky and his productions at the Moscow Art Theatre.

Tairov aimed at creating an 'emancipated theatre' serving exclusively the needs and aims of the actor. He maintained that the actor makes his effect on the audience not by speech and gesture but by his whole personality. 'In order to experience an emotion that is "true to life" one must *not* be an actor – actual experience and stage emotion are two very different things.' To achieve this the actor had to have total mastery over his body and could not leave the expression of his emotion to chance.

New methods of staging had to be devised for this new emphasis on the actor. Tairov treated the stage as one total space. Doing away with conventional scenery such as wings and backcloths, he broke up the flat floor into different levels and rediscovered the three-dimensional stage.

Alexandra Exter was the right designer to realize Tairov's ideas. She developed a whole range of variously coloured cubist shapes such as cones, pyramids, columns and rostra of various sizes, and flights of steps which helped the 'disintegration of the stage picture' and revealed the 'theatrical truth.'

Don Juan

Opera Ballet by Christoph Willibald Gluck
Project for the Städtischen Bühnen, Cologne, 1929

49
Alexandra Exter

(1882–1949)

Design for a male costume
Pencil and bodycolour
Signed in ink Alex Exter
542 × 285
(E.1597–1953)
Lent by the Department of Designs, Prints and Drawings

Provenance
Given to the Victoria and Albert Museum by Simon Lissim in memory of the artist

Literature
Reade, Brian, *Ballet Designs and Illustrations 1581–1940*, (London, 1967), p. 54, ill. no. 167
Salmina-Haskell, Larissa, *Catalogue of Russian Drawings in the Victoria and Albert Museum*, (London, 1972), p. 17, ill. no. 46

'In her costumes she has an extraordinary capacity for preserving the flavour of a place or an epoch in the midst of vigorous formal constructions.'
James Laver, 'The Theatrical Designs of Alexandra Exter', *Claridge Gallery Catalogue* 1928

'Confronted by opinions expressed, advice given, criticism, sound and interesting ideas interspersed with half-baked and plain silly ones, the designer has to distinguish between these; know when to argue and when to keep quiet; guard against praise, which can be very seductive and convenient but not necessarily justified. He has to create an envelope – provide an atmosphere – that serves the author, the director – focuses on the actor by letting him belong to the environment and the environment to him – *he* is the most important person of all. For the designer to succeed requires a pronounced critical faculty, for he must also remain true to himself as a creative artist. So that when I said the designer is very alone, it is that in the final analysis the decisions are his. It is entirely a matter of decisions; the quality and appropriateness of the design is dependent on these. Therein lies the difficulty – to recognize the right decision.'
Ralph Koltai, 'Theatre Design – The Exploration of Space'

The explorations Ralph Koltai makes are in the mind. He looks for appropriate signs in the text and then creates theatrical reality with symbols. The essence of his reality is metaphorical – 'Does', he asks, 'The Forest of Arden of *As You Like It* actually *have* to be a forest at all?'

As You Like It

by William Shakespeare
Director: Clifford Williams
Designer: Ralph Koltai
Lighting: Robert Ornbo and
John B. Read
Composer: Marc Wilkinson
Principals:
Duke Senior: Paul Curran
Jaques: Robert Stephens
Orlando: Jeremy Brett
Touchstone: Derek Jacobi
Rosalind: Ronald Pickup
Celia: Charles Kay
Phoebe: Richard Kay
Audrey: Anthony Hopkins
National Theatre (Old Vic),
3 October 1967

50
Ralph Koltai

(born 1924)

Costume design for Ronald Pickup
as Rosalind

Silver paint and collage
Signed Koltai, dated 67
520 × 256
(S.1927–1986)

Provenance
Given by the Arts Council of Great
Britain

As can be seen from the cast list this is a design for the controversial all-male production, whose artistic aim was to rediscover the theatrical ambiguities that were well understood by Elizabethan audiences.

The collage of the girls' face is like a metaphor because it is a design for a girl being played by a man, but as it is deliberately not a photograph of Ronald Pickup it is more interesting than if it were a painted face.

'Against Ralph Koltai's set of abstract elegance where the wintry sky is a canopy of crinkly sugar icing and where the trees are graceful Perspex tubes, the courtship of Orlando and Rosalind is wittily played out.'
Milton Shulman, *Evening Standard*, 4 October 1967

But symbols do not always work for everybody:
'Ralph Koltai's plastic decor – dangling transparent tubes and dappled overhead cut-outs, and a variety of silver boots, PVC macs, and tattered regimentals – may relate to modern costume; but it is hard to see what contact they have with an Arcadia, whether sweet or bitter.'
Irving Wardle, *The Times*, 4 October 1967

Even so Koltai won the London Drama Critics' Award for Designer of the Year.

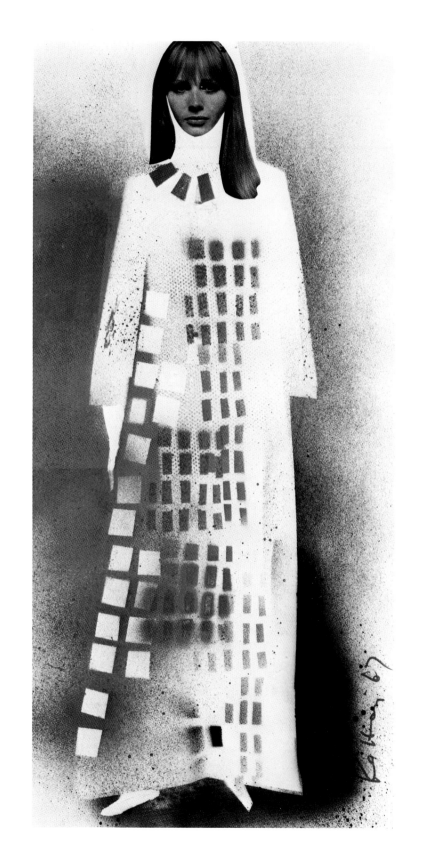

Curtains and cloths

Designs for sets are drawings to be interpreted in three dimensions. The designs in this section are drawings for enlargement in two dimensions. Several different kinds of curtain and cloth may be used in the theatre. First there is a safety curtain which provides a solid fire barrier between the stage and the auditorium; then there is the main curtain or 'house tabs', often of red velvet and split in the middle to allow for individual curtain calls. For some years it has been the fashion to dispense with the house tabs. The audience comes into the auditorium and sees the first set long before it is properly lit and before any action takes place, thereby killing any sense of anticipation and excitement it may have. I think much of the magic of theatre is destroyed by not hearing the sound of the swish of the curtain as it rises in darkness and feeling the draught of cool air from the stage. The so-called drop curtain (see Leslie Hurry's design for *Swan Lake* [No. 5]) is immediately behind the house tabs and is used to set the mood of the piece. Sometimes this is already revealed and I think that is permissable. The so-called front cloth (for *As You Like It* by Claud Lovat Fraser [No. 52]) can be set a little up-stage to allow action to take place in front of it while a set can be changed behind. A back cloth (as Maurice Utrillo's for the ballet *Barabau* [No. 80]) is self-explanatory and might only have a cyclorama or sky cloth behind it. 'Interlude cloth' (as for *Peter Grimes* by Tanya Moiseiwitsch [No. 53]) is not a specific theatrical term but was used here because the opera has a number of musical interludes; it is therefore the same as a drop curtain. There can also be painted gauzes which look solid when lit from in front but vanish when the set behind is lit, and cut cloths which are used for (overhead) borders and (side) wings.

The set for *Giselle* by James Bailey [No. 20] was made using a combination of different kinds of painted cloth.

Le Lac des Cygnes (*Swan Lake*)

Ballet in four acts by Piotr Ilyich Tchaikovsky
Conductor: Constant Lambert
Choreographers: Marius Petipa and Lev Ivanov
Producer: Nicholas Sergeyev revised by Ninette de Valois
Designer: Leslie Hurry
Principals:
Prince Siegfried: Robert Helpmann
The Princess-Mother: Joy Newton
Odette/Odile: Margot Fonteyn
Von Rothbart: Nigel Desmond
Company: Sadler's Wells Ballet
New (now Albery) Theatre,
7 September 1943

51
Leslie Hurry
(1909–78)

Design for the drop curtain
Pencil, pen and ink and watercolour laid on card
Signed in ink Leslie Hurry and dated 1943
330 × 610
(S.32–1982)

Provenance
John Lehmann
Browse and Darby Ltd.

Exhibitions
London, Browse and Darby, *Leslie Hurry – Artist of Dream & Theatre*, 3–27 June 1981, no. 6
Colchester, The Minories, *Leslie Hurry*, 24 October–29 November 1987, no. 95

Literature
Beaumont, Cyril W. and Browse, Lillian (editor), *Leslie Hurry, settings & Costumes for Sadler's Wells Ballets* (London, 1946), ill. pl. 33
Lindsay, Jack, *Paintings and Drawings by Leslie Hurry* (London, 1950) ill. no. 31 p. 54
Girling, Linda and Armstrong, John Hurry, *Leslie Hurry* [catalogue] (Colchester, England, 1987) ill. p. 8

'His original plan was to present all his scenes within a permanent false proscenium frame, eliptical in shape and formed from two swans with their wings outspread. Something of this conception is reflected in the design for the unused drop-curtain, an omission to be regretted for it has many pleasing touches, particularly the symbolic owl with its baleful eyes, seen perched on the shoulder of a swan. But the director of the company, Ninette de Valois, was opposed to this plan on the ground that the swans *depicted* might detract from the swans *represented* by the dancers.'
Cyril W. Beaumont, *Leslie Hurry*

As You Like It
by William Shakespeare
Director: Nigel Playfair
Composer: Arthur Bliss
(arrangements from Elizabethan
sources)
Designer: Claud Lovat Fraser
Principals:
Duke/Frederick: William J. Rea
Jaques: Herbert Marshall
Touchstone: Nigel Playfair
Rosalind: Athene Seyler
Shakespeare Memorial Theatre,
Stratford-upon-Avon, 23 April 1919

52

Claud Lovat Fraser

(1890–1921)

Design for the front cloth
Pencil, crayon and watercolour
Signed in ink C L Fraser fecit
Inscribed 'Before Celia's Cottage
Front cloth'
165 × 190
(S.1398–1986)

Provenance
Sotheby's, London

'*As You Like It* raised a storm at Stratford, which, in those days, was used only for productions of the utmost dingy realism. Local taste found Lovat's gay interpretation of fifteenth-century fashions, and his decorative and completely unrealistic scenery, outrageous and denounced it loudly as 'Futuristic' . . . It is today (1969) almost impossible to realise what a storm of venemous anger this production raised.'
Grace Lovat Fraser, *Claud Lovat Fraser*

The production was revived at the Lyric Theatre Hammersmith, London, on 21 April 1920. The following note on the production by Nigel Playfair was slipped into the programme: 'The costumes have been carefully copied from Missals and Tapestries of the early Fifteenth Century, and are correct in every detail. The scenery is designed as a decorative background for them, and no attempt has been made to achieve an impossible realism.'

But it managed to be a very 1920s fifteenth century.

Before Celia's Cottage.   Front Cloth.

137

Peter Grimes

Opera in a prologue and three acts
by Benjamin Britten
Libretto by Montague Slater based
on George Crabbe's poem 'The
Borough' (1810)
Conductor: Karl Rankl
Director: Tyrone Guthrie
Designer: Tanya Moiseiwitsch
Principals:
Peter Grimes: Peter Pears
Ellen Orford: Joan Cross
Auntie: Edith Coates
Swallow: Owen Brannigan
Royal Opera House, Covent Garden
6 November 1947

53

Tanya Moiseiwitsch

(born 1914)

Design for an interlude cloth
Pen and ink, pencil, chalk, gouache
and watercolour
425 × 595
(Circ.73–1954)

Provenance
Given by the artist
Association of Theatrical Designers
and Craftsmen
Circulation Department Victoria and
Albert Museum

Exhibition
London, Victoria and Albert
Museum, *Modern British Stage
Design*, November 1951–January
1952, no. 53 (subsequently on tour)

This design was for the first revival. The first performance of the opera, also with Joan Cross and Peter Pears, had taken place at Sadler's Wells Theatre, London, on 7 June 1945 to mark the re-opening of the theatre after the war.

'The work itself is the most impressive of Britten's operas, and – though sinister and night-marish rather than, properly speaking, tragic – it undeniably achieves a poetic effect. The feeling of an hallucination was the aim of the production, which was in this respect a triumph.'
R. C., *Daily Telegraph*, 7 November 1947

139

Costume for dancers

Male dancers in Diaghilev's Ballets Russes

When the Ballets Russes first astonished the West in 1909 the amazing and original sets and costumes, in colour ranges previously unseen on the stage, were designed by Russian painters: Alexandre Benois [Nos 33 and 54], Léon Bakst [Nos 55, 65, 74], Nicolas Roerich, Valentin Serov, Boris Anisfeld, Natalia Gontcharova [No. 12], Michel Larionov [No. 89] and others.

Later, when the Ballets Russes were exiled in the West during the First World War, Diaghilev commissioned Western painters: Pablo Picasso [No. 56], Georges Braque, Henri Matisse, Giorgio de Chirico [No. 58], Robert Delaunay, André Derain, Marie Laurençin, Juan Gris [No. 57], Joan Miró and others.

Diaghilev died in Venice in 1929 and his legacy is the art of ballet. Simply stated, ballet continues because of Serge Lifar in Paris at the Opéra, Ninette de Valois in London at Sadler's Wells which led to The Royal Ballet, George Balanchine in New York which led to the New York City Ballet, and Marie Rambert with Ballet Rambert.

Diaghilev's legacy is also a new vision of the art of theatre as seen by the artists he commissioned and whose influence continues.

The Theatre Museum has a number of important designs that were made for the Ballets Russes and this first group concentrates on costumes for the male dancer, a category treated with great originality by Diaghilev's designers.

The coloured gouache version of this design by Pablo Picasso (see No. 56b) became a kind of emblem for the Ballets Russes, and was later also used by Serge Lifar both for the poster for the commemorative Diaghilev exhibition in Paris in 1939 which he organized and for the cover of his biography of Diaghilev. The final costume, worn by Massine, which later belonged to Lifar, is in the collections of Theatre Museum.

Petrushka

(See No. 33 for first production details)

54

Alexandre Benois

(1870–1960)

Costume design for Petrushka
Pencil and watercolour
Signed Alexandre Benois
Inscribed '"Pétrouchka"',
'Pétrouchka (Nijinsky)'
302 × 235
(S.1812–1986)

Provenance
Arnold Haskell
Given by the Arts Council of Great
Britain

Exhibitions
? London, Arthur Tooth & Sons
Ltd., *Alexandre Benois*, 24 June–17
July 1937, no. 21
London, National Gallery, *Ballet
Design*, 3–31 October 1943, no. 18
Edinburgh, College of Art, *The
Diaghilev Exhibition*, 22 August–
11 September 1954, no. 31
London, Forbes House, *The
Diaghilev Exhibition* 3 November
1954–16 January 1955, no. 35
Venice, Palazzo Grassi, *Omaggio ai
Disegnatori di Diaghilev*, 15 June–14
September, 1975, no. vii
Paris, Centre Culturel du Marais,
*1909–1929 Les Ballets Russes de
Diaghilev*, 29 November 1977–17
March 1978, no. 89

Literature
Schouvaloff, Alexander and
Borovsky, Victor, *Stravinsky on
Stage*, (London, 1982), ill. p. 55
Beaumont, Cyril W., *Five Centuries
of Ballet Design*, (London, 1939),
another version illustrated p. 114

Petrushka is probably the most famous ballet produced by Diaghilev because it entered into the repertory of most major dance companies. Between 1911 and 1957 Benois designed fourteen different productions. They are all broadly similar in style and so it is often difficult to specify the particular production and date the drawings. The costume designs for the Ballerina and Petrushka himself cause special problems. Karsavina and Nijinsky so identified themselves with the parts in Benois' mind, and were so successful in their original interpretations, that he often used to inscribe later drawings 'Karsavina' or 'Nijinsky' as here. Sometimes he even dated them '1911'. Most of the original designs for the first production are inscribed and signed in Russian and are in Russia. Some later drawings were never made for productions but for exhibitions or as presents for friends.

This design is, therefore, not for the first production. It could be for the production by the Ballets de Monte Carlo which was first performed at the Alhambra, London, on 15 May 1936 with Vera Nemtchinova as the Ballerina, Anatole Wiltzak as Petrushka, André Eglevsky as The Moor and Nicolas Zverev as The Showman.

If this design was indeed for the 1936 production then it is very likely that it was exhibited at Arthur Tooth & Sons in 1937 along with the designs for the Showman, the Ballerina and the Moor, (nos 22, 23 and 24 in that exhibition) which are also in the collection of the Theatre Museum.

"Pétrouchka"

Pétrouchka
(Nijinsky)

Alexandre
Benois

Le Dieu Bleu (*The Blue God*)

Ballet in one act by Jean Cocteau
and Federigo de Madrazo
Composer: Reynaldo Hahn
Conductor: Désiré-Emile
Inghelbrecht
Choreographer: Michel Fokine
Designer: Léon Bakst
Principals:
The Young Girl: Tamara Karsavina
The Blue God: Vaslav Nijinsky
Théâtre du Châtelet, Paris, 13 May
1912

55
Léon Bakst

(1866–1924)

Costume design for the Young Rajah
Pencil, watercolour and gouache
laid down on card
Signed Bakst, dated 1911
Inscribed 'Dieu Bleu', 'jeunes Rajas'
285 × 210
(S.338–1981)

Provenance
Sir Philip Sassoon
John Carr Doughty Collection
Sotheby's London
Purchased with a grant from the
Linbury Trust

Exhibitions
London, Fine Art Society, *Drawings
of Léon Bakst*, 1912, no. 21
London, Claridge Gallery, *Memorial
Exhibition of Russian Ballet Art*,
March 1930, possibly no. 31 (noted
as *Le Dieu Bleu* from Sir Philip
Sassoon)
Arts Council tour, *Ballet Designs
from the Collection of John Carr-
Doughty*, 1952, no. 5
Edinburgh, College of Art, *The
Diaghilev Exhibition*, 22 August–
11 September 1954, no. 78
London, Forbes House, *The
Diaghilev Exhibition*, 3 November
1954–16 January 1955, no. 92

Literature
Alexandre, Arsène and Cocteau,
Jean, *The Decorative Art of Léon
Bakst*, (London, 1913), ill. pl. 1
Schouvaloff, Alexander 'Show
Business' *Connaisance des Arts*,
Paris, March 1983, ill. p. 68
Schouvaloff, Alexander, 'Theatre
Design: perfect witness of its time'
Antique Collector, (London,
December 1983), ill. p. 93

This is one of the finest and most delicate drawings by this artist, yet it is only for a very minor character.

Parade

Ballet in one scene by Jean Cocteau
Composer: Erik Satie
Conductor: Ernest Ansermet
Choreographer: Leonide Massine
Designer: Pablo Picasso
Principals:
The Chinese Conjuror:
Leonide Massine
The Acrobats: Lydia Lopokhova
and Nicolas Zverev
The American Girl:
Marie Chabelska
The French Manager:
Léon Woizikovsky
The American Manager:
Statkiewitz
Théâtre du Châtelet, Paris, 18 May
1917

56

Pablo Picasso

(1881–1973)

a   Costume design for Leonide
    Massine as the Chinese Conjuror
    (back view)
Pencil
Signed Picasso
275 × 190
(S.374–1985)

Provenance
Leonide Massine
Sotheby's, New York

This previously unpublished
drawing is one of many designs
Picasso made for this costume, but
it was not used.

b   Costume design for Leonide
    Massine as the Chinese Conjuror
    (front view)
Pen and ink
Signed in pencil Picasso
265 × 196
(S.562–1983)

c   Costume design for Leonide
    Massine as the Chinese Conjuror
    (back view)
Pencil
Signed in pencil Picasso
261 × 195
(S.562a–1983)

Provenance
Leonide Massine
Sotheby's London

Literature
Cooper, Douglas, *Picasso Théâtre*
(Paris, 1967), b ill. pl. 79, c ill. pl.
81
Zervos, Christian, *Pablo Picasso,
Supplément aux Années 1914–1919*,
vol. 29, (Paris, 1975), b ill. no. 252,
p. 104
Rogers, Jean Scott, *Stage by Stage*
(London, 1985), b ill. pl. 17, p. 37
Schouvaloff, Alexander, 'Theatre
Design: perfect witness of its time,
Antique Collector, (London,
December 1983), b ill. p. 93
Schouvaloff, Alexander, *The
Theatre Museum* (London, 1987), b
ill. p. 89

Parade was Picasso's first work for the theatre.

Léon Bakst wrote in the souvenir programme of the Ballets Russes for 1917: 'Voici
la *Parade*, ballet cubiste, paradoxal peut-être pour les myopes – vrai pour moi. Picasso
nous donne une vision à lui d'un tréteau de foire, où les acrobates, chinois et managers
se meuvent dans un kaléidoscope, à la fois réel et fantastique . . . Ce grand peintre a
trouvé encore une branche de son art. C'est un décorateur – aussi. Le sentiment de la
mesure le guide ici comme ailleurs.' ('Here is *Parade*, a cubist ballet, paradoxical perhaps
for the short-sighted – truthful for me. Picasso gives us his vision of a fair-ground where
acrobats, chinese conjurors and managers move in a kaleidoscope which is at once both
real and fantastical . . . This great painter has found another branch to his art. He is
also a theatre designer. He is guided here as elsewhere by his feeling for the limits of
possibility.')

Parade was certainly a cubist ballet, and Picasso gave cubism a theatrical application
with his famous 'constructed' costumes for the two Managers. It was also certainly a
revolutionary ballet for the West, but his cubist theories had already been applied to
the theatre a few years earlier by Alexander Tairov and his designer Alexandra Exter
(see No. 49) at the Moscow Chamber Theatre.

Daphnis and Chloé

Ballet in three scenes by Michel
Fokine after pastoral by Longus
Composer: Maurice Ravel
Choreographer: Michel Fokine
Designer: Léon Bakst
Juan Gris (new costume for
Daphnis)
Principals:
Daphnis: Anton Dolin
Chloe: Lydia Sokolova
Darkon: Léon Woizikovsky
Opéra, Monte Carlo, 1 January 1924

57

Juan Gris

(1887–1927)

Costume design for Anton Dolin as
Daphnis
Pencil and watercolour
Signed Juan Gris and dedicated 'A
Doline (*sic*) bien amicalement'
Inscribed 'Tunique en blanc chaud
agrafée à l'épaule droite avec une
rose noire, serré à la taille en
découvrant la hanche droite. Pointe
retournée de la même étoffe bordé
de noir comme la tunique sur le coté
gauche. Culotte très courte et
collante en peau gris bleue.
Genouillière droite et sandales de la
même peau et couleur.' ['Tunic in
warm white gathered at the right
shoulder with a black rose, tight at
the waist revealing the right thigh.
Fichu inside of the same material
bordered with black as the tunic on
the left side. Very short clinging
pants in grey-blue leather. Sandals
in the same leather and colour']
358 × 305
(S.42–1976)

Provenance
Sir Anton Dolin
Sotheby's, London

Exhibitions
London, Claridge Gallery, *Memorial
Exhibition of Russian Ballet Art*,
March 1930, no. 73
Edinburgh, College of Art, *The
Diaghilev Exhibition*, 22 August
–11 September 1954, no. 319
London, Forbes House, *The
Diaghilev Exhibition*, 3 November
1954–16 January 1955, no. 362
Paris, Centre Culturel du Marais,
*1909–1929 Les Ballets Russes de
Diaghilev*, 29 November 1977–17
March 1978, no. 208

Literature
Buckle, Richard, *In Search of
Diaghilev*, (London, 1955), ill. pl. 43

Juan Gris designed a new costume for Anton Dolin for the revival of the ballet by
Diaghilev's Ballets Russes. The other costumes and the sets were still those designed by
Léon Bakst for the first production with Vaslav Nijinsky as Daphnis, Tamara Karsavina
as Chloé and Adolph Bolm as Darkon at the Théâtre du Châtelet, Paris on 8 June 1912.

tunique en blanc chaud
agrafée a l'épaule droite
avec une rose noire, serrée
a la taille en découvrant
la hanche droite. Pointe retour
de la même étoffe bordée de
noir comme la tunique sur
le coté gauche. Culotte très courte et collante
en peau gris bleuté. Genouillère
droite et sandales de la même
peau et couleur.

A Voline bien amicalement
Juan Gris

Le Bal

Ballet in two scenes by Boris
Kochno after a story by Vladimir
Sologub
Composer: Vittorio Rieti
Conductor: Marc-César Scotto
Choreographer: George Balanchine
Designer: Giorgio de Chirico
Principals:
The Lady: Alexandra Danilova
The Young Man: Anton Dolin
Opéra, Monte Carlo, 9 May 1929

58
Giorgio de Chirico

(1888–1978)

Costume design for Anton Dolin in
the *pas de trois Espagnol*
Pencil and watercolour
Signed G. de Chirico
Inscribed on original mount 'Given
by Serge Diaghilev to Georges
Balanchine to Frederick Ashton'
278 × 203
(S.445–1979)

Provenance
Sir Frederick Ashton
Christie's, London

Exhibitions
London, Victoria and Albert
Museum, *Spotlight*, 8 April–26 July
1981, no. 125
Rome, Galleria Nazionale d'Arte
Moderna, *Giorgio de Chirico*,
11 November 1981–3 January
1982, no. 74

Literature
Strong, Roy *et al*, *Designing for the
Dancer*, (London, 1981), ill. p. 88

De Chirico combined fantasy with surrealism: the dancers were disguised as columns, capitals and other architectural elements. The body was asked to become something else. When the body became the sole instrument for dance, costume design for modern ballet eventually developed into nothing but all-over tights for the male dancer, and sometimes not even that.

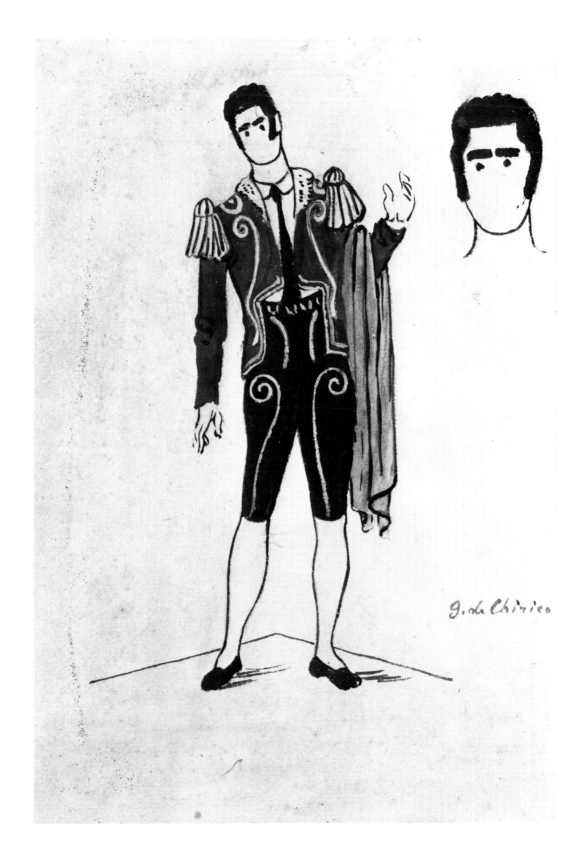

Ballerinas

'You cannot dress up a ballerina as a historically accurate Greek or Egyptian maiden, a lady of the seventeenth century, a marquise of the eighteenth, and then add to the whole the ballet shoe. The result would be ugly and absurd. To soften this absurdity, to transform the ugly into the elegant, one must resort to further concession, to compromise, and as a result of these concessions, there arises a whole series of standards. It was out of these standards that there grew up the canons of the ballerina's costume. The frock must be lifted high enough from the ground to permit the movement of the legs to be seen; this frock must be made of very light material so that it does not impede the action, or weigh down. These standards led to the creation of the special ballet frock, called a *tu-tu*, made of tarlatan and gauze. This frock grew longer or shorter but throughout all its changes it continued to resemble the calyx of a flower and lent the ballerina her specific form. A ballerina is a girl whose feet are clad in heelless shoes, around whose legs are flesh coloured tights, extending to the waist, around which is placed something akin to a fleecy cloud.'

Alexander Benois quoted in Cobbett Steinberg *The Dance Anthology*

59
Studio of Louis René
Boquet
(1717–1814)

Costume design for a princess,
c.1750
Pen and watercolour over pencil
178 × 215
(E.6–1956)

Lent by the Department of Designs,
Prints and Drawings

Literature
Laver, James, *Costume in the Theatre*, (London, 1964), ill. p. 144
Reade, Brian, *Ballet Designs and Illustrations 1581–1940*, (London, 1967), p. 19, ill. pl. 62
de Marly, Diana, *Costume on the Stage 1600–1940*, (London, 1982), ill. p. 90 no. 59

The original drawing for this subject is in the Bibliothèque de l'Opéra, Paris and shows two figures. This appears to be a contemporary replica made in the studio of Boquet, possibly for use in the wardrobe workshop, and is of the left-hand figure only. James Laver described designs by Boquet as being 'fantastications of contemporary dress.' This costume is certainly not very practical to dance in.

*The Truth about the
Russian Dancers*

Fantasy in one act by J. M. Barrie
Composer: Arnold Bax
Conductor: Alfred Dove
Choreographer: Tamara Karsavina
Designer: Paul Nash
Principals:
Lady Vere: Gertrude Sterroll
Lord Vere: Basil Foster
Karissima: Tamara Karsavina
London Coliseum, 15 March 1920

60

Paul Nash

(1889–1946)

a Costume design (wedding dress)
   for Tamara Karsavina as
   Karissima
Signed with monogram PN
Inscribed 'Original sketch design
for a dress for Mdme Karsavina
Truth about the Russian Dancers.
Coliseum, London, 1920'
Signed on mount by Tamara
Karsavina

b Costume design (golf costume)
   for Tamara Karsavina as
   Karissima
Signed with monogram PN, dated
1920
Inscribed 'Original sketch for a
golfing costume/Madame Karsavina/
Truth about The Russian Dancers'
Signed on mount by Tamara
Karsavina

Both pen and ink and watercolour
248 × 150 (each drawing)
(S.550.1980 & S.549.1980)

Provenance
John Carr Doughty

Exhibitions
London, Victoria and Albert
Museum, *International Theatre
Exhibition*, 3 June–16 July 1922,
possibly included in no. 86A
(catalogued as four designs in one
frame)
London, National Gallery, *Ballet
Design*, 3–31 October 1943, no. 115
(a) and (b)
Arts Council tour 1952, *Ballet
Designs from the Collection of John
Carr-Doughty*, nos 52 and 53
London, Victoria and Albert
Museum, *Spotlight*, 8 April–26 July
1981, no. 197 (60a only exhibited)

Literature
Bottomley, Gordon, 'The Theatre
Work of Paul Nash', *Theatre Arts
Monthly*, New York, January 1924,
vol. viii no. 1, pp. 38–48
Buckle, Richard, *Spotlight* (London,
1981) [catalogue], p. 56

'Although the piece does not work as an intelligent piece of writing it lends itself to interpretation by a combination of rare ability, all touched by the new influence. There is
Barrie, turned Diaghileff admirer, Karsavina, the Diaghileff leading lady, Arnold Bax,
a Diaghileff composer, and Paul Nash, an extremist painter, possessed of the ability and
the particular kind of imagination necessary to turn out settings and costumes that receive
the Diaghileff blessing.'
Huntly Carter, 'About the Theatre in London', *Theatre Arts Magazine*, July 1920

Original sketch design
for a dress for
Mme Karsavina
Truth about the
Russian Dancers.
Coliseum, London
1920.

Original sketch design
for a Golfing costume
Madame Karsavina
Truth about
The Russian
Dancers.

A Tragedy of Fashion (or
The Scarlet Scissors)

Ballet by Ashley Dukes, as part of
revue *Riverside Nights* by A. P.
Herbert and Nigel Playfair
Composer: Eugene Goossens
('Kaleidoscope')
Conductor: Alfred Reynolds
Choreography by Frederick Ashton
Principal dancers:
Monsieur Duchic: Frederick Ashton
Orchidée (his partner): Marie
Rambert
Lyric Theatre, Hammersmith,
15 June 1926

61

Sophie Fedorovitch

(1893–1953)

a   Costume design for Marie
    Rambert as Orchidée
Pencil, watercolour and gold paint
355 × 215

b   Projected costume design for
    Marie Rambert
Pencil and watercolour
Inscribed 'silver', 'silver', 'back'
315 × 220
(S.887/8–1983)

Provenance
Dame Marie Rambert Bequest

Exhibition
London, Victoria and Albert
Museum, *Sophie Fedorovitch*, 1955,
no. 2 (61a only)

Literature
Rambert, Marie, *Quicksilver*
(London, 1972), pp. 119–23

This was Frederick Ashton's first ballet. Marie Rambert wrote: 'Now came the question of décor and costumes. Again Fred wanted to do what Diaghilev had done for *Le Train Bleu* – have them designed by Chanel. Again I had to disappoint him, for two reasons: not only could we not afford Chanel, but even if we could I did not want a dressmaker – however brilliant for fashion clothes – to design stage costumes. I suggested Sophie Fedorovitch. She immediately produced beautiful designs of the right character and a perfect set . . .'

'She had a marvellous clarity of eye, and eliminated everything from her final designs but the bare, beautiful bones of her inner vision . . . But the work on paper was not the whole of Sophie. She was a perfectionist, and the final achievement was not reached until she saw, with the rise of the curtain, what she had so triumphantly imagined.'
Siriol Hugh Jones, *Sophie Fedorovitch* in unidentified periodical

Fedorovitch designed eleven ballets for Frederick Ashton.

Symphonie Fantastique

Choreographic symphony in five
tableaux after the programme by
Hector Berlioz
Composer: Hector Berlioz
Choreographer: Leonide Massine
Designer: Christian Bérard
Principals:
Tamara Toumanova
Leonide Massine
Marc Platov
George Zorich
Colonel de Basil's Ballets Russes
Royal Opera House, Covent Garden,
24 July 1936

62
Christian Bérard
(1902–49)

Costume design for Tamara
Toumanova as The Beloved in scene 2
Watercolour heightened with white
Signed Bérard
305 × 228
(S.516–1980)

Provenance
John Carr Doughty

Exhibitions
London, National Gallery, *Ballet
Design*, 3–31 October 1943, no. 44
London, Victoria and Albert
Museum, *Spotlight*, 8 April–26 July
1981, no. 148

Literature
Amberg, George, *Art in Modern
Ballet*, (London, 1946), ill. no. 63
Buckle, Richard, *Spotlight* (London,
1981) [catalogue], ill. no. 148, p. 45
Strong, Roy *et al*, *Designing for the
Dancer* (London, 1981), ill. p. 71

'Everything depends on a sense of theatre . . . That is why it is important to be experienced and to know what 'works' in the theatre.

Colour is a very important element, but I think you must be cautious when using it. It can help a great deal, but it can also do a lot of harm. Too much colour can distract an audience from listening to the play. A sense of colour – like architecture – is innate, and you must be guided by the play.'
Christian Bérard in *Labyrinthe*, Paris, 1950 quoted by Boris Kochno

Les Patineurs

Ballet in one act
Composer: Meyerbeer arranged by
Constant Lambert
Conductor: Constant Lambert
Choreographer: Frederick Ashton
Designer: William Chappell
Principals:
Margot Fonteyn
Robert Helpmann
Vic-Wells Ballet Company
Sadler's Wells Theatre,
22 September 1937

63
William Chappell

(born 1909)

Costume design for Margot Fonteyn
in the *pas de deux*
Pencil, watercolour and silver paint
Signed Chappell
Inscribed 'high neck white fur',
'white hat very small with shallow
crown net draped back over crown
big char (?) of net with floating
end', 'skirt (circular) sleeves (bit leg
of mutton), polonaise bustle & hat
trimming of white net with biggish
white spots (size of a shilling)',
'white fur', 'white satin bodice
trimmed silver braid as many row of
diamond buttons down centre', 'Pas
de deu (*sic*) & girl in white', 'draped
up bustle bow with ends tra(iling)',
'white fur round arm holes'
Signed by Margot Fonteyn
395 × 258
(S.534–1980)

Provenance
John Carr Doughty

'Mr Frederick Ashton's new ballet . . . is a divertissement set on a skating rink in Vienna. In movement and colour it is delightful, and Mr William Chappell's costumes are brilliantly part of the scene of gay animation.'
The Sunday Times, 21 February 1937

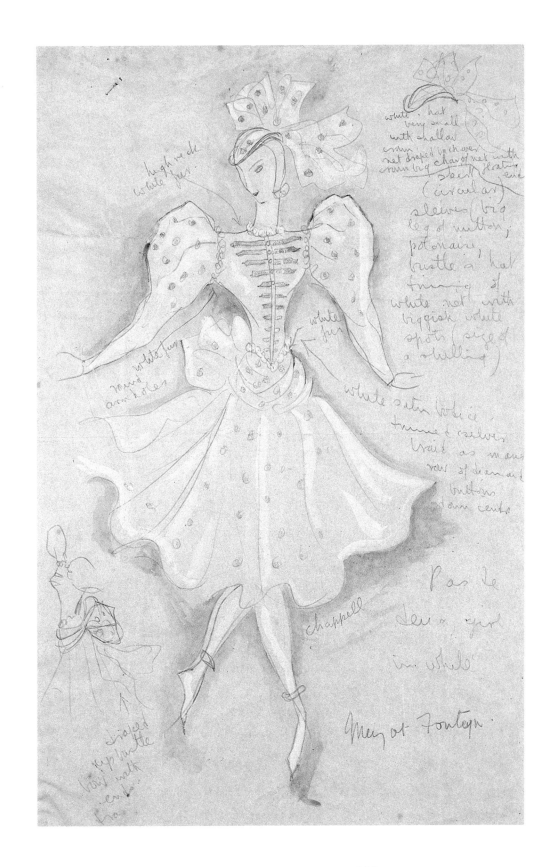

Act II

VERIGO
ODILE

162

Swan Lake

Ballet in four acts
Composer: Peter Ilyich
Tchaikovsky
Conductor: Mark Ermler
Choreographer: Marius Petipa and
Lev Ivanov produced by Anthony
Dowell with Act I waltz by David
Bintley
Designer: Yolanda Sonnabend
Principals:
Odette/Odile: Cynthia Harvey
Prince Siegfried: Jonathan Cape
Princess: Deanne Bergsma
Von Rothbart: Derek Rencher
The Royal Ballet
Royal Opera House, Covent Garden,
12 March 1987

64
Yolanda Sonnabend

(born 1935)

Costume design for Cynthia Harvey
as Odette/Odile in Act II
Pencil, pen and ink, watercolour
and glitter
Signed Y Sonnabend
Inscribed 'Odette, as Pavlova swan
only one with wider shape', 'white
panel overlapped', 'pleats sequin at
top', 'veiled/OD Odile'
460 × 335
(S.485–1989)

Provenance
The artist
Given by The Linbury Trust

'When I am designing I am less aware of seeing as a painter, though painting must have an effect on my work. Increasingly I have found myself drawn by the practical and structural problems of making sets and costumes. This engineering process is essential to the poetic. The discipline of the designer is demanding in that the artist has to submit to the vision of a Mozart or a Chekhov and the director's concept. After the arduousness of solving a set, designing costumes follows fluently.'
Yolanda Sonnabend in Bryan Robertson (*et al*) *Yolanda Sonnabend*

—

'When the skirt, for the purpose of displaying the legs, is shortened to the degree that it resembles an open parasole, I claim that this is unsightly and that poetry and beauty have been sacrificed for acrobatics.'
Michel Fokine, *Memoirs of a Ballet Master*

P.S. Ballet costume has been described as 'Nudity tempered by the suggestion of a period.'

163

Furniture and properties

'The supreme accomplishment of the stage designer is the creation of a complete unit of colour and design – costumes, properties, scenery and lighting – so that as far as the *visual* basis of the stage picture is concerned, it is under the control of one man.'
Herman Rosse, 'The Stage Designer', *Theatre Arts Monthly*, May 1924

Furniture and 'props' can be bought at auction, hired from antique shops or specialist theatrical stores. Good property masters have a 'nose' for where the right things are to be found, but often a designer will insist that the only thing that will fit his scheme is one designed by him and specially made. There are two examples here, one for furniture and one for props. Bakst's design [No. 65] served as an instruction to the stage carpenter with details about the curtain rail as well as directions to the property master. Audrey Cruddas [No. 66] shows the careful attention that a designer should give to every object seen on stage.

Le Spectre de la Rose

Ballet in one scene by Jean-Louis
Vaudoyer from the poem by
Théophile Gautier
Composer: Carl-Maria von Weber
(*Invitation to the Waltz*)
orchestrated by Hector Berlioz
Conductor: Nicolas Tcherepnine
Choreographer: Michel Fokine
Designer: Léon Bakst
Dancers:
The Young Girl: Tamara Karsavina
The Rose: Vaslav Nijinsky
Diaghilev's Ballets Russes
Opéra, Monte Carlo, 19 April 1911

65
Léon Bakst

(1866–1924)

Design for stage furniture:
armchair, harp, curtain rail, bed
Pencil, watercolour, gouache and
gold paint
Signed in ink Bakst
Inscribed '*Spectre de la Rose*', '3
barres en bronzes avec colliers' [3
brass rails with rings], '*3 rideaux* en
tule (*sic*) moucheté de soie blancs
(2 rideaux pour les deux fenetres) et
un large rideau pour le lit caché
dans la niche. Ces rideaux viennent
d'un seul coté' [3 curtains in white
silk spotted tulle (2 curtains for the
two windows) and a large curtain
for the bed concealed in the niche.
These curtains only draw from one
side], 'hauteur de la fenetre et du lit'
[height of the window and the bed],
'1 objet' (3 times), 'taile d'homme'
(3 times) [human height], '1 lit avec
3 coussins avec dentelle/draps et
couverture soie' [1 bed with three
lace cushions/silk sheets and
blanket], 'Harpe en bois de rose et
or (style 1820–40)' [Rosewood and
gold harp (style 1820–40)]
398 × 265
(S.1004–1984)

Provenance
Serge Lifar
Ader, Picard, Tajan (Commissaires-
Priseurs), Paris

Exhibitions
London, Forbes House, *The
Diaghilev Exhibition*, 3 November
1954–16 January 1955, no. 87
Strasbourg, Ancienne Douane, *Les
Ballets Russes de Serge de Diaghilev
1909–1929*, 15 May–15 September
1969, no. 109
Venice, Palazzo Grassi, *Omaggio ai
Disegnatori di Diaghilev*, 15 June–
14 September 1975, no. vi
Norwich, University of East Anglia,
Sainsbury Centre for Visual Arts,
The Diaghilev Ballet in England,
11 October–20 November 1979 (and
London, The Fine Art Society,
3 December 1979–11 January 1980),
no. 25

Literature
Buckle, Richard, *In Search of
Diaghilev* (London, 1955) ill. pl. 16
p. 17

Bakst made two designs for the stage properties, this one and one with a birdcage, chest
of drawers, table and sofa. They show with what care he treated every detail of the
production.

'Unheralded by quarrels, demure as it should be, the *Spectre de la Rose* gently passed
over the agony of the first night. That night there was no fuss on the stage – Diaghileff
benign; only Bakst moved about, helpless, agitated, carrying a canary cage. The cage
was a feature of the scenery from his point of view, a nuisance from everybody else's.
He had installed the canary over a window from where it had been banished; Nijinsky
had to appear through it, and the other window was to be free for Nijinksy's famous
leap. "Levoushka, for God's sake, chuck the canary, the public is growing impatient.
Oh, don't be ridiculous; canaries don't stand on chest of drawers." – "You don't understand, Serioja; we must give the atmosphere." Bakst protracted the interval alarmingly,
but he gave the atmosphere by finally hoisting the canary high up under a cornice. In
further travel the cage, with its stuffed bird, was maliciously lost.'
Tamara Karsavina, *Theatre Street*

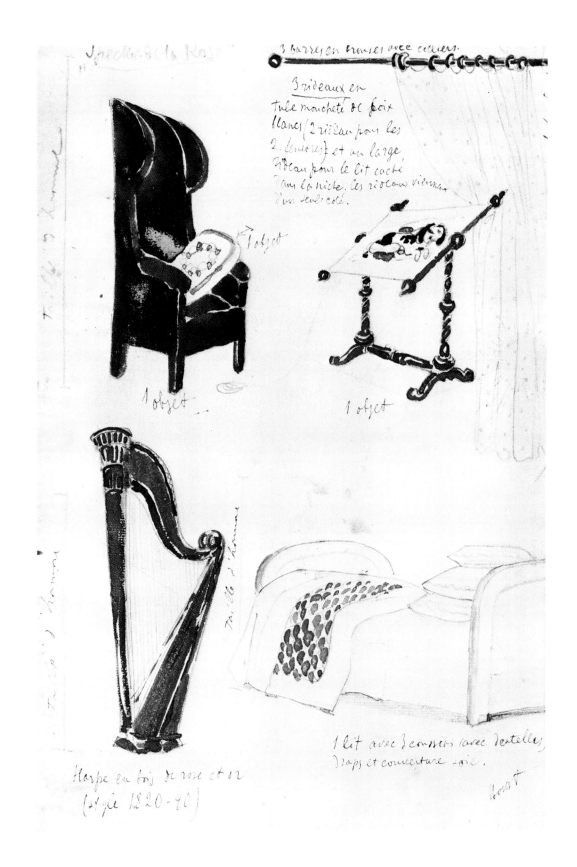

Spectacle de la Rose

3 barres en travers avec coliers.

Rideaux en
tule moucheté de poix
blancs (2 rideau pour les
2 fenêtres) et un large
rideau pour le lit caché
dans la niche. les rideaux viennent
d'un seul coté.

1 objet

1 objet

1 objet

Harpe en bois de rose et or
(style 1820-40)

1 lit avec 2 coussins avec dentelles,
draps et couverture soie.

Macbeth

by William Shakespeare
Director: Michael Benthall
Designer: Audrey Cruddas
Principals:
Macbeth: Paul Rogers
Lady Macbeth: Ann Todd
Banquo: Eric Porter
Old Vic Theatre, 9 September 1954

66

Audrey Cruddas

(1914–79)

Designs for stage properties

a a standard
Inscribed 'flat to resemble pewter bound with lead on one side only', '*one standard* with two flags torn and ragged', 'one as above', and with measurements denoting feet
210 × 139

b horse skeleton
Inscribed '"*Macbeth*"', '*Painted Horse Skeleton*'
78 × 257

c drapes for banquet
Inscribed 'same as standard without flag', '*Painted Drapes for Banquet*' and with measurements denoting feet
150 × 221

d cushion, sceptres, orbs, looking glass
Inscribed 'two cushions for crowns', '*Macbeth Props*', 'Double Orbs', 'Two Scepters (*sic*), '2 double orbs', '3 single orbs', 'no cushion' and with measurements denoting feet and inches
223 × 269

All pencil and gouache
(S.899/902–1982)

Provenance
The estate of the artist
Miss Mary Cheseldene

'A peculiarity of Miss Cruddas's designs is that, unlike those of many of her colleagues – in which the most summary indications of the set or costumes are given in a calligraphic shorthand – her own drawings for the theatre are executed in a loving and meticulous detail.'

Colin MacInnes, *Great Bardfield Artists*

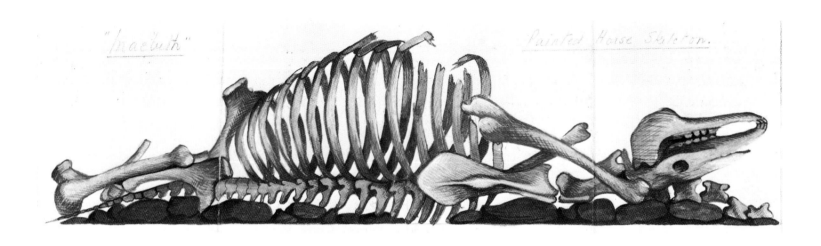

"Macbeth"   Painted Horse Skeleton.

Painted Drapes for Banquet

2ft 6"

Two Cusions for crowns

1'6"

5'

6"

Macbeth
Props.

Double Orbs

2ft

3'6"

4'6"

2 Double orbs

Two Sceptas

3 Treble sceptas
from three

3 Swords

Themes and variations

Costumes for Gilbert and Sullivan operas

Certain traditions can develop in costume design, so that the basic idea of a costume for a character is repeated from production to production with only minor alterations. The classic example of this is the costume for the character of Harlequin (see No. 91). He began with a costume that was all rags and tatters which then became stylized into multi-coloured diamond shapes and finally into blocks of colour. There is, of course, a limit to the variation to the style of costume for the characters in the plays of say Chekhov or Oscar Wilde because of the specific period and place; although there was recently a production of *The Seagull* set in contemporary Ireland.

The D'Oyly Carte company, under the supervision of Gilbert himself, specified at the beginning how the operas should be produced and how they should be designed. The management remained faithful to the first ideas and so each new production was really a re-production aiming to maintain the tradition. Thus, successive designers had to work within fairly strict definitions. But changing fashions, not just in clothes but in design generally, obviously affect and influence a designer. This series of drawings shows how several designers have produced different solutions to the problems posed by costuming the same characters in two of the operas – *The Mikado* [Nos 67–69] and *The Gondoliers* [Nos 70–73]. The two operas are quite different in style and character, but in each case I have included an example of a design from the first production, one by Charles Ricketts who did a lot to revitalize the productions in the 1920s and, in the case of *The Gondoliers*, designs from the 50s and 60s to show the progression in changing fashion, while keeping to the original mood.

I am especially grateful to Catherine Haill for her help in cataloguing this group of designs.

The Mikado, or the Town of Titipu

Opera set in Japan in two acts
Composer: Arthur Sullivan
Librettist: W. S. Gilbert
Conductor: François Cellier
Directors: Arthur Sullivan and
W. S. Gilbert
Designers: Hawes Craven (sets),
Wilhelm (male costumes)
Principals:
Nanki-Poo: Durward Lely
Ko-Ko: George Grossmith
Pooh-Bah: Rutland Barrington
Yum-Yum: Leonora Braham
Savoy Theatre, 14 March 1885

67

Wilhelm (alias William
John Charles Pitcher RI)
(1858–1925)

Costume design for Durward Lely as
Nanki-Poo in Act II
Watercolour and bodycolour over
pencil on card
Signed and dated 'Wilhelm/85'
Inscribed 'Lely'
228 × 190
(M.3)

Provenance
Given by Dame Bridget D'Oyly
Carte

WILHELM.
85.

The Mikado

(see previous entry for main credits)
Designer: Herbert Norris

68

Herbert Norris

(died 1950)

Costume design for Nanki-Poo in
Act II
Pencil and watercolour, pen and ink
on card
Signed and dated 'Herbert Norris
1921'
Inscribed 'Nanki Poo Act II'
380 × 270 overall, 330 × 230 image
(M.23)

Provenance
Purchased from the artist by the
D'Oyly Carte Company, 1923
Given by Dame Bridget D'Oyly
Carte

This was a design for a projected new production in 1921.

The Mikado
(see No. 67 for main credits)
Conductor: Malcolm Sargent
Director: Rupert D'Oyly Carte
Designer: Charles Ricketts RA
Principals:
Nanki-Poo: Charles Goulding
Ko-Ko: Henry A. Lytton
Pooh-Bah: Leo Sheffield
Yum-Yum: Elsie Griffin
New production: Princes Theatre
(now Shaftesbury), 20 September
1926

69

Peter Goffin FRSA
(1906–1974)

after Charles Ricketts RA
(1866–1931)

Costume design for Thomas Round
as Nanki-Poo in Act II
Costumier's copy
Inscribed 'sash white red dot', 'red/
black/white mid', 'bright red dots',
'pink', 'red middle as under
kim(ono) pink', 'under kim(ono)
mid red pink', 'green black centre',
'skirt dots middle out edge broken',
'mid skirt dis', 'Mr Thomas Round',
and inscribed by Peter Goffin 'The
Mikado', 'Nanki-Poo/Act II', 'copy
of original drawing by
Ricketts/P.G.58'
475 × 305 overall, 375 × 273 image

Provenance
Given by Dame Bridget D'Oyly
Carte

Ricketts always insisted on retaining his original designs, copies of which remained in
the wardrobe of the company and were updated from time to time. When Peter Goffin re-
designed the composite sets in 1957, he also updated some of the costume designs including
this one for Nanki-Poo which Thomas Round first played at Sadler's Wells Theatre in 1947.

The Mikado

Nanki-Poo
Act II

Mr Thomas Round

*The Gondoliers or, The King
of Barataria*

Comic opera in two acts
Composer: Arthur Sullivan
Librettist: W. S. Gilbert
Conductor: François Cellier
Directors: W. S. Gilbert and Arthur
Sullivan
Designers: Hawes Craven (sets);
Percy Anderson (costumes)
Principals:
The Duke of Plaza-Toro:
Frank Wyatt
Don Alhambra del Bolero:
W. H. Denny
Marco Palmieri: Courtice Pounds
The Duchess of Plaza Toro:
Rosina Brandram
Savoy Theatre, 7 December 1889

70

Percy Anderson
(1851–1928)

Costume design for Decima Moor as
Casilda in Act II (with insert detail
of head-dress)
Inscribed 'Act II', 'Carlotta (crossed
out)', 'Casilda', 'see back', 'nothing
round throat', 'no train'
Inscribed on reverse with notes and
sketches relating to costume
252 × 176
(GN.10)

Provenance
Given by Dame Bridget D'Oyly
Carte

The Gondoliers

(See previous entry for main credits)
Conductor: Malcolm Sargent
Director: Rupert D'Oyly Carte
Designer: Charles Ricketts RA
Principals:
The Duke of Plaza-Toro:
Henry A. Lytton
Don Alhambra del Bolero:
Leo Sheffield
Marco Palmieri: Derek Oldham
The Duchess of Plaza Toro:
Bertha Lewis
New production: Savoy Theatre, 21
October 1929

71

after Charles Ricketts RA

(1866–1931)

Costumier's copy of costume design
for Winifred Lawson as Casilda in
Act II
Watercolour and bodycolour over
pencil on photochemical copy
Inscribed 'Casilda II Act', 'Miss
Lawson', 'train 3½ yds', 'Duchess
4½', 'Rose', 'out'
293 × 250
(GN.104)

Provenance
Given by Dame Bridget D'Oyly
Carte

(See also No. 69.)

The Gondoliers

(See No. 70 for main credits)
Conductor: Isidore Godfrey
Designer: Peter Goffin
Principals:
The Duke of Plaza-Toro: Peter Pratt
Don Alhambra del Bolero: Kenneth Sandford
Marco Palmieri: Thomas Round
The Duchess of Plaza-Toro:
Ann Drummond-Grant
New production: Princes Theatre (now Shaftesbury), 15 December 1958

72

Peter Goffin FRSA

(1906–1974)

Costume design for Jennifer Toye as Casilda in Act II
Pencil and watercolour
Signed 'Goffin/58'
Inscribed 'Casilda Act II'
Inscribed and stamped on reverse
373 × 261
(GN.174)

Provenance
Given by Dame Bridget D'Oyly Carte

Casulana
Act II

Gatti/64

The Gondoliers

(See No. 70 for main credits)
Conductor: Isidore Godfrey
Director: Anthony Besch
Designer: Luciana Arrighi
Principals:
The Duke of Plaza-Toro: John Reed
Don Alhambra del Bolero: Kenneth
Sandford
Marco Palmieri: Ralph Mason
The Duchess of Plaza-Toro:
Christine Palmer
New production: Saville Theatre,
29 January 1968

73
Luciana Arrighi

(born 1942)

Costume design for Valerie
Masterson as Casilda in Act II (and
Christine Palmer as the Duchess of
Plaza-Toro)
Pen and ink and watercolour with
swatches
Inscribed and signed later 'Sketch
by Luciana Arrighi'
Inscribed 'Act II Casilda & Duchess
of Plaza-Toro', 'Stiff satin ribbon',
'white mousseline', 'Heavy silk
cloak – double row satin tassell (*sic*)
edge', 'Edging ruched satin', 'white
chiffon', 'taffeta with double row
tassels'
385 × 250

Provenance
On loan from the Trustees of the
D'Oyly Carte Company

ACT-II
CASILDA &
DUCHESS OF PLAZA-TORO.

STIFF SATIN
RIBBON

HEAVY
SILK
CLOAK-
DOUBLE
ROW SATIN
TASSELL
EDGE

EDGING
RUCHED
SATIN

WHITE CHIFFON.

TAFFETTA WITH DOUBLE ROW
TASSELS

Multiple costumes for groups, choruses and crowds

One of the frequent practical problems for a designer to solve is how to design costumes for groups, choruses and crowds. The effect on the stage of the whole group has to be sensed. Sometimes, especially in ballet, the same costume is made for the whole group (as Bakst's design for sixteen men in a cake-walk, [No. 74]), a *corps de ballet* or a line of chorus girls in a revue where the theatrical effect comes precisely from the uniformity. It would be unrealistic, and so quite wrong, for choruses in opera and crowds in plays to be identically dressed, even when the actors are apparently uniformly costumed in evening dress, as Dobujinsky's chorus in *War and Peace*, [No. 75] or in 'historical' dress, as the townsmen in *Gismonda* designed by Thomas [No. 76] – the variations of detail help to animate the crowd.

Hullo, Tango!

Revue in nine scenes by Max Pemberton and Albert P. de Courville
Composer: Louis A. Hirsch
Lyricist: George Arthurs
Designer: Léon Bakst (costumes)
Principals:
Ethel Levy
Shirley Kellog
Harry Tate
George W. Monroe
London Hippodrome, 23 December 1913

74
Léon Bakst

(1866–1924)

Costume design for sixteen men in the cake-walk in scene 8: *Pavillion (sic) Armenonville, Paris*
Pencil, watercolour and gold paint laid down on card
Signed Bakst, dated 1913
Inscribed '*Cake-walk* 16 *hommes*', '*étoile sur les revers du pantalon et sur les manchettes*' ['star on trouser turn-up and on cuffs']
440 × 273
(S.508–1980)
Inscribed on sheet stuck on reverse of card '*Cake-walk* – (Pavillon Armenonville) 16 costumes *d'hommes*',
'*Chapeau haute forme* en feutre grisbleu (*pas* en soie!) avec bande grisbleu et bleu foncé en soie dur et mat faisant carrés.'
['Top hat in grey-blue felt (not silk) with a band of blue-grey and dark blue silk alternately shiny and matt forming a pattern of squares']
'*Perruque blonde-cendrée* cheveux raides et lisses.'
['Ash-blond wig straight sleek hair']
'*Maquillage rouge* vineux, basané, à l'americaine.'
['Red winy make-up, suntanned American style]
'*Monocle*'

'*Habit bleu* en drap bleu avec col en velour, boutons hémisphères nickel. Manches assez étroites.'
['Blue coat of blue cloth with velvet collar, hemispherical nickel buttons. Tight sleeves']
'*Chemise de couleurs* (copier très exactment la nuance) avec des boutons de manchettes en forme d'étoile ameriquaine (*sic*).'
['Coloured shirt (copy the shade exactly) with cuff buttons like an American star']
'*Cravatte avec franges*, noeud gros, dessins imprimés sur un (*sic*) laine très fine ou belle cachemire.'
['Necktie with fringe, large knot, printed design on very fine wool or cashmere']
'*Gilet* en velour *noir*-bleu avec 1 bouton en nickel hémisphère.'
['Velvet blue-black waistcoat with 1 hemispherical nickel button']
'*Pantalon* en drap très fin – rouge vermillon – militaire, avec revers en bas, recouverts d'étoiles americains imprimés en jaune *très foncé* sur fond noir.'
['Trousers in very fine cloth – vermilion red – military, with turn-ups covered with printed American stars in very dark yellow on black background']

'*Gants vert cru* plus grand que la main d'artiste.'
['Crude green gloves larger than the artist's hand']
'*Chaussettes en* soie, imprimée de la nuance sur blanc.'
['Silk socks printed with colour shade on white']
'*Souliers vernis* noirs forme américaine. *Demandez au régisseur*, s'ils ont de semelles qui claquent?'
['Black polished American-style shoes. Ask the director if they have soles which clatter?']
Signed 'L. Bakst'

Provenance
John Carr Doughty

'He took more trouble than most designers, for he went over to Paris, picked out all the materials and arranged in the actual workshops how the costumes were to be made. The result was extremely satisfactory, and *Hullo, Tango* was one of the most artistically costumed shows with which I have been associated.'
Albert de Courville, *I Tell You*

War and Peace

Opera in five acts and thirteen
scenes by Serge Prokofiev and Mira
Mendelson based on the novel by
Leo Tolstoy
Composer: Serge Prokofiev
Project for the Metropolitan Opera
House, New York, 1947 and
possibly for Boston, 1950

75
Mstislav Dobujinsky

(1875–1957)

Costume designs for the chorus in
the ball scene
Pencil and watercolour
Signed with monogram, dated 1950
Inscribed 'War & Peace', 'Ball VI',
'18', 'Boston'
256 × 382
(S.67–1987)

Provenance
Gabrielle Enthoven Collection

(See also No. 31.)

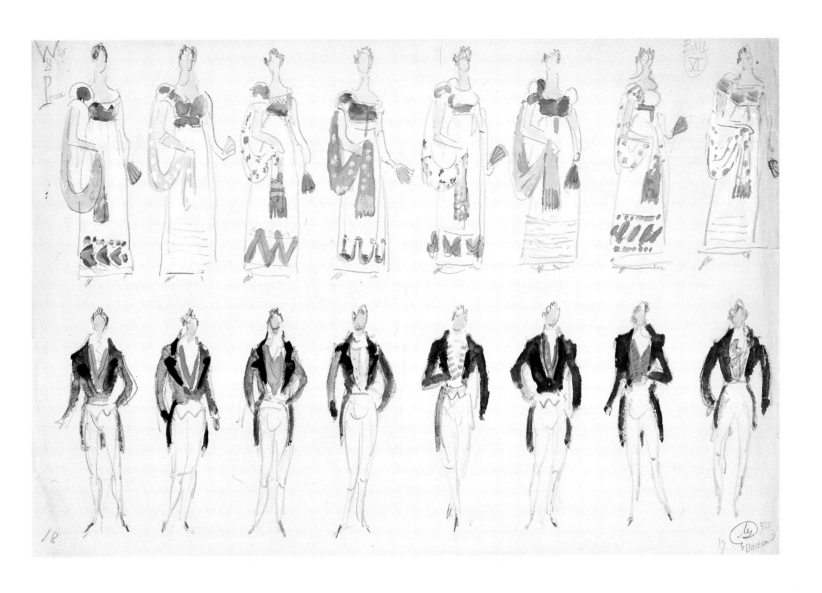

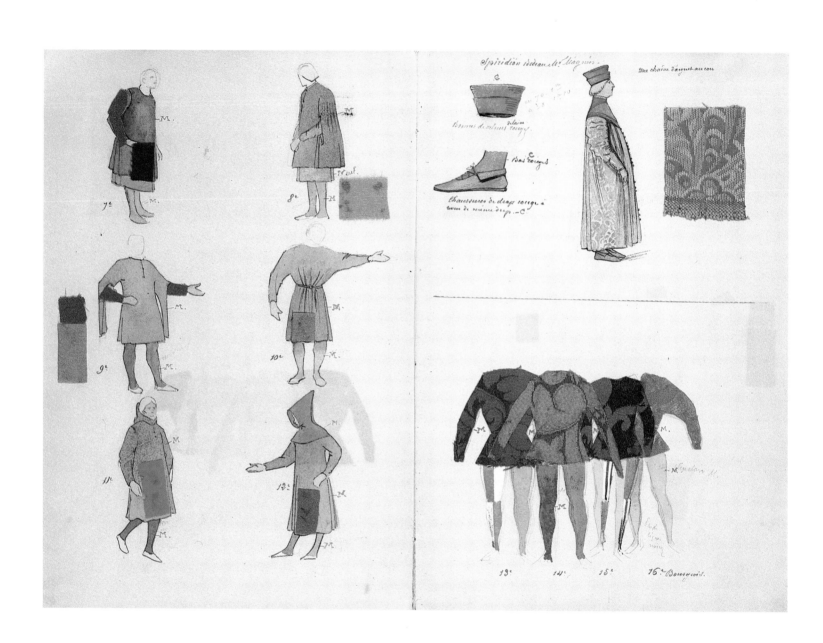

Gismonda

Drama in four acts and five tableaux
by Victorien Sardou
Directors: Henry E Abbey and
Maurice Grau
Principals:
Gismonda: Sarah Bernhardt
Almerio: Lucien Guitry
Théâtre de la Renaissance, Paris,
31 October 1894

76
Théophile Thomas

(*c*.1846–1916)

Costume designs for M. Magnin as
Spiridion Bedeau and ten townsmen
Two pages from a book of sketches
Pencil, pen and ink, watercolour
and appliqué material
Inscribed 'Spiridion Bedeau M
Magnin', 'une chaine d'argent au
cou' (silver chain round neck),
'Bonnet de velours rouge, bas
rouges, chaussures de drap rouge à
revers de même drap' (Red velvet
hat, red stockings, shoes of red
material with lining of the same
material), and the code letters 'M',
'N' and 'C' (apparently M = from
stock, N and C = to be made).
375 × 260 size of each page of book
(S.608–1983)

Provenance
Sotheby's, London

Working it out

This section shows some of the different stages and processes involved in making a design for the theatre; it is working things out on paper and expressing ideas in two dimensions which are then visualized in three.

King Arthur and the Knights of the Round Table

'Chivalric entertainment' in three
acts by Isaac Pocock
Composer: T. Cooke
Designers: Messrs Andrews,
Franklin and Clarkson Stanfield
(sets); Mr Palmer and Mrs Coombe
(costumes)
Principals:
Arthur: Charles Diddear
Merlin: Mr Younge
Sir Roland: T. P. Cooke
Gyneth: Miss Clifton
Morgana La Faye: Mrs Vining
Theatre Royal, Drury Lane,
26 December 1834

77

Isaac Pocock

(1782–1835)

a Set design for Act I, scene 1 'Hall
in the castle of Sir Roland'
139 × 190

b The same at the appearance of
Morgana La Faye and the Magic
Horse
137 × 189

Pencil, pen and ink and watercolour
Inscribed a) '1st scene 1st act',
b) '1st scene 1st act upon
appearance of Morgana'
(S.47–1987)

Provenance
Gabrielle Enthoven Collection

Exhibitions
Bonn, Rheinisches Landesmuseum,
June–July 1979
Sunderland, Museum and Art
Gallery, *The Spectacular Career of
Clarkson Stanfield 1793–1867*, 1979,
no. 74 a & b

Literature
van der Merwe, Pieter (*et al*), *The
Spectacular Career of Clarkson
Stanfield 1793–1867, Seaman, Scene-
Painter, Royal Academician*,
(Sunderland, 1979) [catalogue]
pp. 64–5

Pieter van der Merwe has re-attributed these drawings; previously they were thought
to be by Clarkson Stanfield, but now they are considered to be by the writer of the
play showing the designer what he had in mind. How far Clarkson Stanfield followed
Pocock's ideas is not known.

A designer always tries to fulfil the writer's intentions, but the writer may not be
the best person to visualize his own intention. This is why hardly any playwright has
been or is a designer, but he can always make suggestions.

78

Anonymous

Set designs for an unidentified
production

Provenance
Sotheby's, London

a cabin trunk closed

b cabin trunk open

c cabin trunk revealing staircases

Each pencil, watercolour and silver
paint

Each 248 × 325
(S.44, 44a, 44b–1976)

These designs are probably for a production at the Folies Bergère, Paris, in the 1930s.
The stage at the Folies Bergère is very shallow so the best way of making the stage look
full of people is by using stairs. This technical device became a famous hall-mark of this
music-hall, and these designs show the scenic development leading up to the grand
entrance of the star at the top of the stairs.

At one time these designs were attributed to Freddy Wittop (born 1911). I am most
grateful to Mr Wittop for the following comment: 'Unfortunately I cannot identify these
drawings with any certainty as we all, designers of that period (like Gesmar [No. 45],
Zig, Shanks, Curti, Dany [No. 43]) and myself, had a sameness in our renderings. Later
we all developed our individual styles. Today the sole survivors of that era are Erté
[No. 42] and myself. Erté kept his style, for which we are all thankful. I evolved – so
these sketches could be mine, but as a rule most of my work bore my signature.'

A Midsummer Night's Dream

by William Shakespeare
Director: Ron Daniels
Designer: Maria Björnson
Choreographer: David Toguri
Puppet Master: Barry Smith
Principals:
Theseus/Oberon: Mike Gwilym
Hippolyta/Titania: Juliet Stevenson
Royal Shakespeare Theatre,
Stratford-upon-Avon, 15 July 1981

79
Maria Björnson
(born 1949)

a Costume designs for Kevin
Wallace and Claire Traverse
Decon as puppeteers
Inscribed '*Puppeteers* Basic
costumes + some theatrical element.
i.e. hat or (woman's) apron or skirt,
man's w.coat or shirt', 'Kevin
Wallace/Claire Traverse Decon/
'MIDSUMMER NIGHT DREAM/
STRATFORD 81', 'net on faces,
nuns veiling shirt', 'crushed velvet
jacket', 'small check', 'satin from
stock', 'mittens', 'satin from stock',
'striped apron/ankle boots'

b Costume designs for Bert
Parnaby as Philostrate, for Mike
Gwilym as Theseus, for Juliet
Stevenson as Hippolyta, and for
John Burgess as Egeus
Inscribed '*Philostrate* 2 stock/shirt
jacket fake w/coat Breeches Boots',
Bert Parnaby, Mike Gwillym (*sic*),
Juliet Stevenson, *Egeus* 2, John
Burgess, stock shirt/or fake w/coat
Jacket breeches Boots', '*Theseus* 2,
The same on 1m.23s change into
this', '*Hippolita* 2 quick change
seconds', 'coat longer', which
boots? Gloves?' ''A MIDSUMMER
NIGHT DREAM' STRATFORD '81''
Each watercolour, gouache, collage
paper and fabric

Each signed Maria Björnson
Each 250 × 405
(S.1174/5–1982)

Provenance
Holsworthy Gallery

Puppeteers
Basic costumes +
some theatrical
element ie hat
or (woman's) apron or
skirt
man's w·coat or
shirt.

Kevin Wallace

Claire Travesse Decon 'MIDSUMMERS NIGHT DREAM'

STRATFORD 81'

net on faces
Nuns veiling shirt
crushed velvet jacket
Borrouck'
small checks

satin from stock
mittens
satin from stock
striped apron
ankle boots

backs
hat

Maria Björnson

W. C. Fields, at the age of 21, earned his living as a juggler. It remained a life-long enthusiasm. He even asked for a juggling sequence to be written into Micawber.

Philostrate ② Bert Parnaby   Mike Gwillym Juliet Stevenson   **Egeus** ②

Stock/shirt
Jacket fake w/coat
Breeches
Boots

② John Burgess

stock
Shirt/or fake
w/coat/
Jacket
Breeches
Boots

Theseus ②
The same on
1m.23s change
into this.

Hippolita ②
quick change
seconds.

which boots?
gloves?

Maria Björnson

coat longer?

'A MIDSUMMERS NIGHT DREAM' STRATFORD '81

Scene painting

There are two methods of scene painting, vertical and horizontal.

In the vertical method, which is usual in England, the canvas is put on a frame which, as the scene is painted, is either gradually hoisted up through a slit in the floor beside the wall, or the painters are hoisted up on a gantry.

In the horizontal method, known also as the 'Continental method', the canvas is painted on any large floor. The main advantage of the Continental method over the vertical, according to Vladimir Polunin, is that it 'renders it possible for the decorator to employ any form of technique, from the opaque colours of tempera and gouache to the transparent washes associated with water-colour; for, since the colours do not trickle down on a horizontal plane, the most delicate *nuances* are possible of achievement.'

Barabau

Ballet in one act
Composer: Vittorio Rieti
Conductor: Roger Desormière
Choreographer: George Balanchine
Designer: Maurice Utrillo
Principals:
Barabau: Léon Woizikovsky
Peasant woman: Lydia Sokolova
Italian sergeant: Serge Lifar
Company: Diaghilev's Ballets Russes
London Coliseum, 11 December 1925

80

Alexandre Schervashidze
(1869–1968)

after Maurice Utrillo
(1883–1955)

a Squared-up drawing of the backcloth
Pencil
Signed A. Schervashidze
Inscribed in pencil 'Barabau', '(illegible) nuzhno napisats derevo' ['. . . must paint the tree'], inscribed in ink 'mise en mètre du rideau de fond "Barabau"' ['Squaring up the backcloth for "Barabau"']
Inscribed on reverse with calculations
165 × 210
(S.186–1978)

Provenance
Sotheby's, London

Exhibition
London, Victoria and Albert Museum, *Images of Show Business*, 17 November 1982–17 April 1983, no. 69 (a)

Literature
Fowler, James (editor), *Images of Show Business* (London, 1982), no. 69

b Squared-up drawing of the ground plan
Pencil and blue ink
Inscribed in Russian and French (top to bottom, left to right) 'Vkhod v tserkov' ['Entrance to church'], 'lesnoi kldn' ['wood flat'], 'ogorod'. ['garden'] chassis, 'dom' ['house'], 'frise', ['border'], 'dereva' ['trees'], 'golub. kul.' ['pale blue wing'], 'frise', 'golub. kul.', 'Echelle 0,1½'
Stamped with Serge Lifar Collection stamp
202 × 257
(S.60–1985)

Provenance
Serge Lifar
Sotheby's, London

'The working drawings are now ready for transference to the canvas. All this is simple, provided the height and width of the sketch are in proportion to those of the stage for which the scenery is intended . . . Return to the canvas which is dry and tempting . . . If the designer's sketch is very complicated, it is advisable to simplify the tracing, choosing the most characteristic lines and masses, for it is easy to lose oneself in a maze of lines on the canvas. It is a distinct aid to indicate the shadows very lightly and then leave the drawing in order to concentrate on the colour scheme.'
Vladimir Polunin, *The Continental Method of Scene Painting*

Both Schervashidze and Polunin were designers as well as scene painters. Between them they painted most of the scenes for Diaghilev's Ballets Russes productions.

Frise au milieu du rideau de fond. Barabau. A. Schawinsky

1 2 3 4 5 6 7 8 9 10

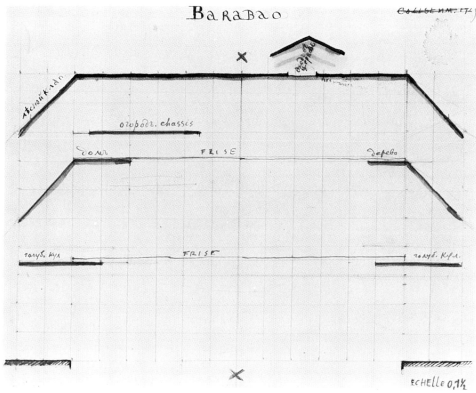

BARABAO   COLLSERM. 174

огородн. chassis

домі   FRISE   дерево

голуб. кул.   FRISE   голуб. крл.

ECHELLE 0,1½

205

Don Giovanni

Opera in two acts
Composer: Wolfgang Amadeus
Mozart
Librettist: Lorenzo da Ponte
Conductor: Fritz Busch
Director: Carl Ebert
Designer: John Piper
Lighting designer: Michael Northen
Principals:
Don Giovanni: Mario Petri
Leporello: Alois Pernerstorfer
Donna Anna: Hilde Zadek
Donna Elvira: Suzanne Danco
Masetto: Geraint Evans
Glyndebourne Opera, 11 July 1951

81

John Piper

(born 1903)

a Sketches for sets
Pencil, pen and ink and watercolour
Inscribed 'Sketches for Don
Giovanni Glyndebourne. 1949'
225 × 321
(S.1766–1986)

b Arch (not used)
Pencil, watercolour, pastel
254 × 350
(S.1773–1986)

c Arch (used)
Pencil, watercolour, pastel
237 × 179
(S.1767–1986)

d Wing (used)
Pencil, gouache, watercolour and
pastel
265 × 156
(S.1769–1986)

Provenance
Given by the artist

'Ebert (the director) had insisted that each scene must have a separate set, and this caused
Piper an extraordinary amount of hard work . . . he came up with a remarkable solution
for the numerous scene changes by designing two large houses in three dimensions in
perspective and set on trucks, which could be moved in various positions on the stage.
In turn they 'married' with the perspective on the backcloth wherever they were placed.
They were very beautiful designs and greatly enhanced the production. An interesting
sideline was the fact that when it came to the lighting, I discovered that any light falling
directly onto the painted scenery destroyed the atmosphere that Piper had intended, so
that I decided that the scenery should be lit entirely from light spilling over from the
acting areas which achieved the effect that Piper wished to create.'
Michael Northen, 'Designs for the Theatre' in David Fraser Jenkins *John Piper*

Sketches for Don Giovanni, Glyndebourne, 1949

10'6"

A poster, programmes and a petition

Designers often like to concern themselves with every aspect of the design of a production: the graphics on posters and programmes are an important element in establishing the mood of a show in the audience's mind. Dudley Hardy [No. 82] was essentially a graphic designer. I have included his drawing both to show that the Theatre Museum is concerned with all the performing arts including the circus, and because it is a most successful example of poster design – clear, uncluttered and to the point. This was for the first poster for the first season for what became England's most famous circus and Hardy boldly used the clown as its universal symbol. Tchelitchew [No. 83], the designer of *Ode* an experimental ballet produced by Diaghilev in 1928, made a number of drawings loosely inspired by Leonardo da Vinci, one of which was used as the design for the cover of the souvenir programme. It seems that people will always find an escape in theatre even when they are trapped in a prisoner-of-war camp. Ronald Searle [No. 84] and his fellow prisoners somehow managed to survive Changi Jail in Singapore by producing pantomimes. The drawing by David Hockney [No. 85] is not a design for the theatre but it became a vital document in helping to safeguard the Theatre Museum.

Bertram Mills' Great International Circus and Fun Fair

Principal acts:
Orlando's Circus Horses
M. Emil Gautier, introducing the Thought-Reading Dog, 'Rex'
Les Frères Plattier
Sanger's Elephants
The Kikuta Troupe
The Five Flying Rixfords
Olympia, London, 17 December 1920

82
Dudley Hardy
(1866–1922)

Preliminary design for the poster and programme cover
Pencil, watercolour and bodycolour
439 × 316
(AHCI.2)

Provenance
Antony Hippisley Coxe Circus Collection

Exhibition
London, Victoria and Albert Museum, *Images of Show Business*, 17 November 1982–17 April 1983, no. 89

Literature
Fowler, James (editor), *Images of Show Business* 5 (London, 1982) no. 89

83

Pavel Tchelitchew

(1898–1957)

Design for a programme cover
Pencil and gouache [oil and conté
crayon]
Signed in ink P. Tchelitchew and
dated 28
316 × 245
(S.34–1976)

Provenance
J. Bonjean
A. Elfer
Sotheby's, London, purchased with
funds given by Richard Buckle

Exhibitions
London, Claridge Gallery, *Paintings
and Drawings by Paul Tchelitchew*,
July 1928, no. 34
Venice, *XVII Espozione
Internazionale d'Arte*, 1930, no. 28
Wadsworth Atheneum
Hanover Gallery

Literature
Buckle, Richard, *In Search of
Diaghilev*, (London, 1955), a similar
design ill. pl. 124 p. 92
*The Serge Lifar Collection of Ballet
Set and Costume Designs*, (Hartford,
Connecticut, 1965), a similar design
ill. no. 178 p. 82

This is a variation of a design for the programme cover for the twenty-first Paris season of Diaghilev's Ballets Russes in 1928. This design has been pinpricked by hand on one of the feet; on the final printed cover the whole body was pinpricked by hand.

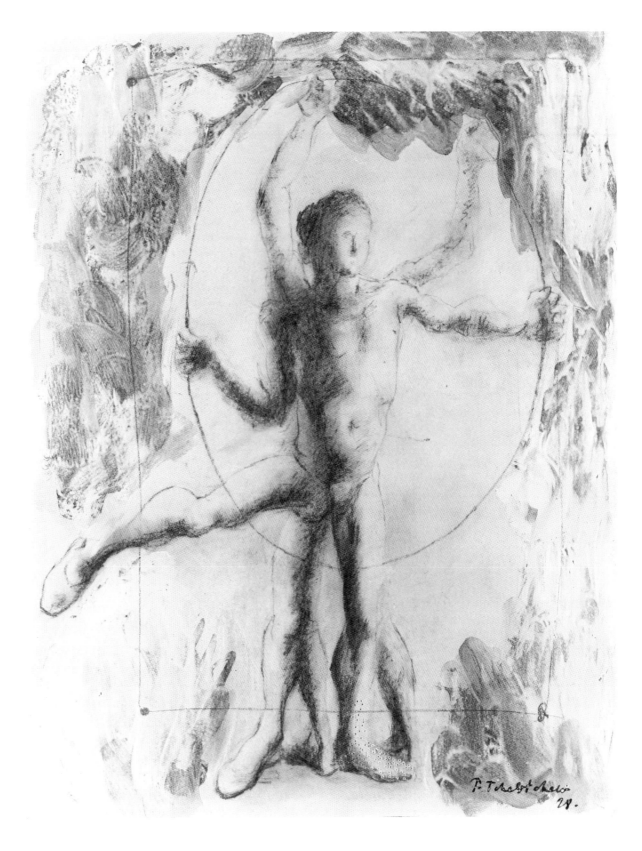

*Cinderella and the Magic
Soya Bean*

Burlesque pantomime by
Alan Roberts
Director: Alan Roberts
Designer: Ronald Searle
Composer: Bill Williams
Principals:
Cinders: John Mackwood
Widow Twankey: Robin Welbury
Court Magician: John Beckerley
The Barn Theatre, Sime Road,
Singapore, 22 February 1944

84

Ronald Searle

(born 1920)

Programme
Pencil, pen and ink and watercolour
Signed Ronald Searle
155 × 95
(S.413–1978)

Provenance
Given by John Beckerley

The Barn Theatre was in Changi Jail, a Japanese prisoner-of-war camp during the Second
World War. Not surprisingly Ronald Searle cannot remember making this drawing, but
the courage, determination and humour needed to create such an entertainment under
the most difficult circumstances are clear to see.

85
David Hockney

(born 1937)

Drawing for a petition to save the
Theatre Museum, 1982
Pen and ink
Signed DH, dated '82
310 × 222

Provenance
Given by the artist to the Theatre
Museum Association

The drawing is of Punchinello, one of the classic characters of the Italian *commedia dell'-arte*. During 1980–81 Hockney had designed *Parade*, a triple bill, for the Metropolitan Opera House, New York and had been much affected by an exhibition he had seen at the Frick Collection of the Punchinello drawings by Giovanni Domenico Tiepolo (1727–1804). He said: 'People have forgotten about such fine drawing. Not even Picasso could draw like that. Those Tiepolos have unbelievable, fantastic life . . . I gave the Met wardrobe people the Tiepolo catalogue.'

In 1982 an official report to the British government recommended that the Theatre Museum project should be abandoned. Considerable public feeling was aroused and 33,000 people signed this petition on behalf of the Museum during June and July. They signed a tear-off slip at the bottom addressed to the Right Hon. Paul Channon PC MP, Minister for the Arts, and kept a reproduction of the drawing. Mr Channon reprieved the Museum in August 1982. Building work started in January 1984, and the Museum opened on 23 April 1987.

This was the text on the back of the petition written by Catherine Haill:

WHO THE THEATRE MUSEUM
Gielgud, Garrick, Grock, Goldoni,
Shakespeare, Schiller, Solti, Shaw,
Terry, Tilley, Thorndike, Tutin,
Beatles, Bernhardt, Barrymore.
WHAT THE THEATRE MUSEUM
Opera, ballet, panto, drama,
Punch and Judy, Columbine,
Photos, playbills, prompt books, models,
Posters, costumes, masks, design.
WHY THE THEATRE MUSEUM
Tourists, children, academics,
Critics, actors in a play,
Grandmas, singers, pop fans, dancers,
All the audience of today.
WHERE THE THEATRE MUSEUM
Locked in basements, attics, cupboards,
Far from any public view,
Help release this great collection
Stored for Britain and for you.

Governments in turn have promised:
'Covent Garden is a must
For your treasures of the theatre' —
Promises soon turn to dust.

You can help save this Museum,
Make the Minister aware;
Sign the slip with name and address —
Parliament must know you care.

SAVE THE THEATRE MUSEUM

Evocations

'As far as I'm concerned, there is no fixed work of art in the theater; every work has to be brought to life by the people doing it.'

David Hockney, *Hockney Paints the Stage*

While, in one sense, this is perfectly true and while Lee Simonson in *The Stage is Set* may say, 'Drawings for the theatre are desires. They should all be signed with a question-mark, for they are, even the best of them, pretences until they are fulfilled,' they both forget that we the spectators need tokens for our memory when the play is over. They forget that sometimes the only important evidence left of an ephemeral performance which has vanished for ever is the 'fixed work of art'. A design is therefore an historical document. While it is true that it can never be a substitute for the whole performance, it should not just be dismissed as being insignificant because of that. The purpose of a design, as we have seen, should be to express the mood, the spirit and the symbolic meaning of the play. Good design achieves its purpose and thereby, I think, becomes a work of art.

For the last group I have brought together six designs which for me impart a particularly forceful sense of the atmosphere of the piece for which they were originally drawn, even though I never saw any of the productions. (The *Pierrot Lunaire* [No. 88] I did see was much later, but in the same set.) These six drawings are not a random choice but I could have chosen others from those in other groups for the same reason.

'The stage setting should tend towards that elusiveness in life found in the rainbow.'

John Wenger, *The Mission of the Stage Setting*

The Midsummer Marriage

Opera in three acts by Michael Tippett
Composer: Michael Tippett
Conductor: John Pritchard
Director: Christopher West
Choreographer: John Cranko
Designer: Barbara Hepworth
Principals:
Mark: Richard Lewis
Jenifer: Joan Sutherland
King Fisher: Otakar Kraus
Bella: Adele Leigh
Royal Opera House, Covent Garden,
27 January 1955

86
Barbara Hepworth

(1903–75)

Costume design for one of the ritual
dancers
Pencil and watercolour
Inscribed in ball point pen 'Ritual
Dancers'
345 × 245
(S.2190–1986)

Provenance
Given by the British Council

The libretto of the opera perplexed the critics, the music pleased them and the designer
was hardly mentioned.

Ruth

Opera in one act
Composer: Lennox Berkeley
Librettist: Eric Crozier
Conductor: Charles Mackerras
Designer: Ceri Richards
Principals:
Naomi: Una Hale
Orpah: April Cantelo
Ruth: Anna Pollock
Boaz: Peter Pears
The Head Reaper: Thomas Hemsley
English Opera Group
Scala Theatre, 2 October 1956

87

Ceri Richards

(1903–71)

Costume design for Anna Pollock as Ruth
Pencil, ink, gouache and watercolour on paper laid down on card
Signed in pencil Ceri Richards, dated August 1956
Inscribed 'preliminary design for Ruth costume for first scene/English Opera Group/October 1956'
284 × 196
(S.28–1982)

Provenance
Mrs Monika Kinley

Ritual
Dancer

Preliminary
Design for
Ruth costume
for first Scene

English Opera Group
October 1956

Ceri Richards
August 1956

Pierrot Lunaire

Ballet by Glen Tetley
Choreographer: Glen Tetley
Composer: Arnold Schönberg
Designer: Rouben Ter-Arutunian
Principal:
Glen Tetley
Institute of Technology, New York,
5 May 1962

88

Rouben Ter-Arutunian

(born 1920)

Set design
Watercolour and gouache
Signed R. Ter-Arutunian
Inscribed '"Pierrot Lunaire" Glen
Tetley Co. 1962/63'
368 × 527
(S.344–1988)

Provenance
Sotheby's, London

'Part of the illusion is conjured up by the visual impact of décor and costumes. Already, by itself, without performers, the décor establishes a definite atmosphere, evokes a mood. No matter whether it is made out of steel pipes, painted floppy canvas, or just two small square blocks that sit on the empty stage. The selection has been by the designer (we hope!), and there it is.'

'Today one is more and more inclined to less décor. One tends to like everything stripped – the stage uncluttered, sufficiently clean and well organized at its periphery, and in the right scale with the character of the work. This, one believes, is the condition most favorable for the performer. But this can be exaggerated to a degree of unimaginative dryness. Then something is missing. The performer is robbed of an important ingredient he could feed upon, another dimension that could have further challenged the involvement of both himself and his audience.'

Rouben Ter-Arutunian, 'In Search of Design', in Cobbett Steinberg *The Dance Anthology*

Le Renard

Burlesque by Igor Stravinsky
Composer: Igor Stravinsky
Conductor: Igor Stravinsky
Choreographer: Serge Lifar
Designer: Michel Larionov
Principals:
Fox: Léon Woizikovsky
Cock: Nicolas Efimov and Louis
Agustino
Ram: Boris Lissanevitch and
Bernardo Agustino
Cat: Jean Hoyer and Adolph
Hierlinger
Diaghilev's Ballets Russes
Théâtre Sarah Bernhardt, Paris,
21 May 1929

89

Michel Larionov

(1881–1964)

Variation on the design for the set
Pencil, watercolour and bodycolour
laid on card
Signed M. Larionow, dated 1921
Inscribed in Russian 'Baika pro lisu
i petukha sotchinenie Igorya
Stravinskago khoreographiya Lifara
dekoratsiya Larionova balet
Diaghileva.' ('The tale of the fox and
the cock by Igor Stravinsky,
choreography by Lifar, set by
Larionov, ballet by Diaghilev.')
510 × 665 (image)
(S.1936–1986)

Provenance
Given by the Arts Council of Great
Britain

'Le décor de ballet n'as pas pour unique objet de situer, conformément aux indications d'un livret, le lieu et l'époque d'une action; la reconstitution scrupuleusement historique de tel ou tel style n'est pas l'objectif qui lui est assigné. Le décor est avant tout une création indépendante, soutenant l'esprit de l'oeuvre à représenter, une forme d'art autonome possédant ses problèmes particuliers et soumise à ses lois propres.'

('Décor for ballet does not have the sole purpose of locating, according to the directions in the libretto, the place and time of the action; the scrupulous historical reconstruction of one style or another is not an aim allotted to it. Décor is primarily an independent creation, maintaining the spirit of the work to be performed, an autonomous art form with its own particular problems and subject to its own laws.')
Nathalie Gontcharova and Michel Larionov, *Les Ballets Russes*

The original production with a similar design but with choreography by Bronislava Nijinska was staged at the Opéra, Paris, on 18 May 1922. Larionov made many versions of the set drawing in the style of a Russian 'lubok' (primitive print), and many of them, like this one, are inexplicably dated 1921. This painting, however, as is obvious from the inscription, was made after Lifar had done new choreography in 1929.

Carmen

Ballet by Roland Petit adapted from
the opera by Meilhac and Halévy,
after Prosper Merimée
Composer: Georges Bizet (selections)
Conductor: Jean Gitton
Choreographer: Roland Petit
Designer: Antoni Clavé
Principals:
Carmen: Renée Jeanmaire
Don José: Roland Petit
Ballets de Paris de Roland Petit
Princes Theatre, (now Shaftesbury),
21 February 1949

90
Antoni Clavé

(born 1913)

Costume design for a whore
Gouache on black paper
360 × 128
(S.478–1989)

Provenance
Roland Petit
Given by Richard Buckle

Exhibition
London, Victoria and Albert
Museum, *Spotlight*, 8 April–26 July
1981, no. 150

Literature
Buckle, Richard, *Spotlight*
[catalogue], (London, 1981), p. 47

'Clavé's sets and dresses were of a colour and fierce fantasy that would have made even
Diaghilev's heart beat faster.'
Richard Buckle, *The Observer*, 27 February 1949

Death in Adagio

Ballet by Keith Lester
Composer: Scarlatti (arrangements)
Choreographer: Keith Lester
Designer: Bernard Meninsky
Principals:
Alicia Markova
Diana Gould
Molly Lake
Markova-Dolin Ballet
New Theatre, Oxford, ?1936

91
Bernard Meninsky

(1891–1950)

Costume design for Harlequin
Pencil and gouache laid down on
card
Inscribed in pencil 'Harlequin' and
?'Haskell'
440 × 335
(S.479–1989)

Provenance
The artist
Given by Richard Buckle

Keith Lester told me: 'The ballet was a murder mystery inspired by the Italian *commedia dell'arte*. It was my attempt to be modern. Alicia had a solo and appeared in a bright gold wig. I think the choreography was fun, but no-one much liked it and it was never done again after Oxford.'

Harlequin remains the symbol of theatre.

Major exhibitions of theatre art in the twentieth century

This is a selected list of some of the more important exhibitions of theatrical art which have taken place in different countries this century. The published catalogues are useful works of reference.

From 1929, when Diaghilev died, there have been a number of exhibitions specifically on the subject of the Ballets Russes. They have included designs but often other documentary material as well.

From 1967 to 1987 Sotheby's held regular sales of theatrical material in London and New York. They were usually devoted to the work of Diaghilev's designers for the Ballets Russes, and the viewing days before the sales provided an opportunity for seeing a large number of different designs. Illustrated catalogues of all the sales were published although the information about the designs is occasionally unreliable.

This list excludes one-man shows and general historical exhibitions.

1900
Paris
Exhibition 1900. Groupe III, Classe 18, Matériel de l'Art Théâtral

1908
April–October
Paris, Louvre, Union Centrale des Arts Décoratifs
Exposition théâtrale

1913
Mannheim, Kunsthalle
Moderne Theaterkunst

1914
Zurich, Kunstgewerbemuseum
Theaterkunst

1919
5–26 April
New York, Bourgeois Galleries
American Stage Designs

1922
Amsterdam, Stedelijk Museum
Internationale Theatertentoonstelling

1922
3 June–31 July
London, Victoria and Albert Museum
International Theatre Exhibition
(The exhibition in Amsterdam was enlarged and transferred to London. It then moved to the Glasgow Art Gallery and Museum at Kelvingrove where it was shown from 22 December 1922–3 February 1923)

1925
Vienna
Internationale Ausstellung neuer Theaterkunst

Paris
Exposition internationale des arts décoratifs et industriels modernes

1926
New York, Steinway Building
International Theatre Exhibition

1927
14 May–2 October
Magdeburg
Deutsche Theater-Ausstellung

London, Victoria and Albert Museum
Modern French and Russian Designs for Costume and Scenery

1928
3 February–3 March
London, Whitechapel Art Gallery
International Theatrical Art

1929
Paris, Musée des Arts Décoratifs, Pavillon de Marsan
Ballets Russes de Diaghilev

November
Barcelona, Duque de la Victoria, Instituto del Teatro Nacional
Congreso y Exposición Internacionales del Teatro

1930
March
London, Claridge Gallery
The Russian Ballet Memorial Exhibition

14–28 October
Paris, Galerie Billiet-Pierre Vorms
Exposition Rétrospective de Maquettes, Décors & Costumes exécutés pour la Compagnie des Ballets Russes de Serge de Diaghilew

1931
25 April–31 May
Zurich, Kunstgewerbemuseum
Theaterkunstausstellung

1933
February–March
Vienna, Künstlerbund Hagen
Der Tanz

Paris, Musée Galliéra
L'Art décoratif au Théâtre et dans la Musique

1934
16 January–26 February
New York, Museum of Modern Art
International Exhibition of Theatre Art

1936
September–October
Vienna, Nationalbibliothek
Internationale Ausstellung für Theaterkunst

1938
June-July
London, The Leicester Galleries
The Dance – An Exhibition of Paintings, Drawings and Sculpture by Artists, Past and Present

1939
March–May
Paris, Musée des Arts Décoratifs, Pavillon de Marsan
Ballets Russes de Diaghilew 1909–1929

1943
5–31 October
London, National Gallery
Ballet Design
(Subsequently toured by CEMA [Council for the Encouragement of Music and the Arts])

1950
London, Victoria and Albert Museum
British Stage Design

1954
22 August–11 September
Edinburgh College of Art
The Diaghilev Exhibition
(This exhibition was enlarged and transferred to London, Forbes House where it was shown from 3 November 1954–16 January 1955)

1955
20 September–5 December
Vienna, Künstlerhaus
Europäische Theaterausstellung von der Antike bis zur Gegenwart

London, Victoria and Albert Museum
French Theatre Art 1935–1955

1956
Los Angeles, County Museum
Costume design for the Theater

1959
22 March–19 April
Indianapolis, Indiana, John Herron Art Museum
50 years of Ballet Designs
(This exhibition was also shown 3–31 May in Hartford, Connecticut, Wadsworth Atheneum, 11 July–16 August in San Francisco, California Palace of the Legion of Honour, and was circulated September 1959–September 1960 by the American Federation of Arts)

New York, Sarah Lawrence College
Design for the Theatre 1934–1959

1961
Zurich, Kunstgewerbemuseum
Oskar Schlemmer und die abstrakte Bühne

1963
Naples
Mostra internazionale de Scenografica Contemporanea

Wiesbaden, Städtisches Museum
Bild und Bühne

1964
4 June–15 August
Zürich, Kunstgewerbemuseum
Das Bühnenbild nach 1945, eine Dokumentation

10 October–22 November
Eindhoven, Stedelijk van Abbe-Museum
Beeldend Experiment op de Planken

1965
Baden-Baden
Bild und Bühne

1966
25 June–17 July
Spoleto, Palazzo Collicola
Tre secoli di Disegni Teatrali

1968
19 November–31 December
London, Grosvenor Gallery
Ballet at the Grosvenor

London, Victoria and Albert Museum
Italian stage designs from the Museo Teatrale alla Scala, Milan

1969
15 May–15 September
Strasbourg, Ancienne Douane
Les Ballets Russes de Serge de Diaghilev 1909–1929

1971
Oslo, Art Centre
Contemporary Theatrical Staging

1974
2 October–2 November
London, Annely Juda Fine Art
Theatre: An exhibition of 20th century theatrical designs and drawings
(This exhibition also toured to Cologne, Galerie Bargera, November–
December 1974; Basel, Galerie Liatowitsch, January–February 1975;
Milan, Galeria Milano, March–April 1975)

1976
7 July–31 October
Munich, Theatermuseum
Bühnenbilder des 20. Jahrhunderts

1977
Cologne, Kunstamt Kreuzberg und Institut für Theaterwissenschaften,
Berlin, Kunstamt Kreuzberg Bonn, Rheinisches Landesmuseum
Theater in der Weimarer Republik

1979
Paris, Bibliothèque Nationale
Diaghilev: Les Ballets Russes

Florence, Belvedere
Visualitá: Bozzetti, figurini e spettacoli 1933–1979

1980
19 January–9 March
San Francisco, Fine Arts Museums
Russian Theater and Costume Designs
(Circulated by The Fine Arts Museums of San Francisco, 1980–82)

10 October–7 December
Hanover, New Hampshire, Dartmouth College Museum and Galleries
Theater Art of the Medici

1981
8 April–26 July
London, Victoria and Albert Museum
Spotlight: Four centuries of Ballet Costume, a tribute to the Royal Ballet

22 May–16 August
Cleveland, Ohio, Cleveland Museum of Art
Art and the Stage

1984
Prato, Palazzo Pretorio
L'avventura del Sipario

16 October–6 January 1985
Detroit, The Detroit Institute of Arts
Designed for Theater

17 November–12 January 1985
Bristol, Arnolfini Gallery
Artists Design for Dance 1909–1984

1984–5
Cologne, Theatermuseum der Universität
Theater Spiegel

1985
10 September–27 April 1986
London, Victoria and Albert Museum, Theatre Museum Galleries
130 set and costume designs from the Theatre Museum

1986
1 March–26 May
Frankfurt am Main, Schirn Kunsthalle
Die Maler und das Theater im 20. Jahrhundert

1987
24 April–2 August
London, Theatre Museum
The King's Pleasures: costume designs for the Court Ballet of Louis XIII

1988
3 September–30 November
McAllen, Texas, McAllen International Museum
Erté and his contemporaries

Moscow, Pushkin Museum
Russkoe Teatralno-Dekoratzionnoe Iskusstvo 1880–1930
(Russian Theatre Design 1880–1930)
from the Collection of Nikita and Nina Lobanov-Rostovsky

1989
17 June–2 July
Granada, Auditorio Manuel de Falla
España y Los Ballets Russes

Select bibliography

Any book on the history of the performing arts, whether it is a general survey or a study of a particular period or country, inevitably touches upon theatre design. This bibliography does not attempt to be comprehensive. It only lists those works (including exhibition catalogues and articles in periodicals, but excluding newspaper reviews) specifically written on the subject of theatre design, and some other books which have been consulted in the preparation of this catalogue.

There are also two indispensable works of reference:

D'Amico, Silvio (editor)
Enciclopedia dello Spettacolo, 9 vols (Rome, 1954–62)

Hartnoll, Phyllis (editor)
The Oxford Companion to the Theatre (London, 1983; 4th edition)
—
Bablet, Denis
Esthéthique générale du décor de théâtre de 1870 à 1914 (Paris, 1965)

Bablet, Denis
Les Révolutions scéniques du XXe siècle (Paris, 1975)

Bablet, Denis *et al*
Die Maler und das Theater im 20, Jahrhundert (Frankfurt am Main, 1986) [catalogue]

Barbey, Valdo
'Les peintres modernes et le théâtre', *Art et Décoration* vol. xxxvii, (Paris, 1920), pp. 97–108, 155–60

Beaumont, Cyril W.
Design for the Ballet (London, 1937)

Beaumont, Cyril W.
Five Centuries of Ballet Design (London, 1939)

Beaumont, Cyril W.
Ballet design past and present (London, 1946) [a combination and extension of the two books above by the same author]

Beaumont, Cyril W. and Browse, Lillian (editor)
Leslie Hurry, Settings & Costumes for Sadler's Wells Ballets (London, 1946)

Benois, Alexandre
Reminiscences of the Russian Ballet (London, 1941)

Beyer, Victor *et al*
Les Ballets Russes de Serge de Diaghilev 1909–1929 (Strasbourg, 1969) [Catalogue of exhibition at the Ancienne Douane]

Blumenthal, Arthur R.
Theater Art of the Medici (Hanover, New Hampshire, 1980) [catalogue]

Blumenthal, Arthur R.
Theater Designs in the Collection of the Cooper-Hewitt Museum (New York, 1986)

Boll, André
Du décor de théâtre (Paris, 1926)

Boll, André
'Wakhevitch and his decors', *World Theatre* vol. 1 no. 3 (Paris, 1951), pp. 41–50

Boll, André
La Décoration Théâtrale (Paris, 1958)

Breitman, Ellen
Art and the Stage (Cleveland, Ohio, 1981) [Catalogue of exhibition at the Cleveland Museum of Art 22 May–16 August 1981]

Buckle, Richard (editor)
The Diaghilev Exhibition (Edinburgh and London, 1954) [catalogue]

Buckle, Richard
In Search of Diaghilev (London, 1955)

Buckle, Richard
Modern Ballet Design (London, 1955)

Castle, Charles
The Folies Bergère (London, 1982)

Clarke, Mary and Crisp, Clement
Ballet Art (New York, 1978)

Clarke, Mary and Crisp, Clement
Design for Ballet (London, 1978)

Cochran, Charles B.
'Stage Decoration and Fantasy', *The Studio* vol. 94 no. 417, (London, December 1927), pp. 392–8

Cogniat, Raymond
Décors de Théâtre (Paris, 1930)

Cogniat, Raymond
Les Décorateurs de Théâtre (Paris, 1955)

Cooper, Douglas
Picasso: Théâtre (Paris, 1967)

Coward, Noël
Present Indicative (London, 1937)

Craig, Edward Gordon
On the Art of the Theatre (London, 1911)

Craig, Edward Gordon
Towards a New Theatre (London, 1913)

de Courville, Albert
I Tell You (London, 1928)

de Marly, Diana
Costume on the stage 1600–1940 (London, 1982)

E.O.H.
'The Art of the Theatre', *The Studio* vol. 83 no. 351, (London, 15 June 1922), pp. 310–18

Fokine, Michele
Memoirs of a Ballet Master (London, 1961)

Fowler, James (editor)
Images of Show Business (London, 1982) [subsequently the catalogue of an exhibition at the Victoria and Albert Museum]

Fraser, Claud Lovat and E.O.H.
'The Art of the Theatre', *The Studio* vol.82 no.334, (London, 15 November 1921), pp.210–15

Fraser, Grace Lovat
Claud Lovat Fraser (London, 1969) [Catalogue of an exhibition at the Victoria and Albert Museum]

Friedman, Martin
Hockney Paints the Stage (New York, 1983)

Fuerst, Walter René and Hume, Samuel J.
XX century stage decoration (London, 1928)

Fülop-Miller, René and Gregor, Joseph
The Russian Theatre (London, 1930; reissued New York, 1968)

Gauthier, Maximilien
'Décors', *L'Art Vivant* (Paris, 1 March 1930), pp.247–8

Gilder, Rosamond *et al* (editor)
Theatre Arts Anthology (New York, 1950)

Gontcharova, Nathalie; Larionov, Michel and Vorms, Pierre
Les Ballets Russes, Serge de Diagilew et la décoration théâtrale (Paris, 1955)

Gropius, Walter and Moholy-Nagy, L. (editors)
Die Bühne im Bauhaus (no. 4 of *Bauhausbücher*) (Munich, 1924)

Gropius, Walter (editor) [translated by Arthur S. Wensinger]
The Theater of the Bauhaus (Middletown, Connecticut, 1961)

Hainaux, René and Bonnat, Yves
Le Décor de théâtre dans le monde depuis 1935 (Brussels, 1956)

Hainaux, René and Bonnat, Yves
Le Décor de théâtre dans le monde depuis 1956 (Brussels, 1964)

Hainaux, René and Bonnat, Yves
Le Décor de théâtre dans le monde depuis 1960 (Brussels, 1964)

Hockney, David see Friedman, Martin

Hogben, Carol (editor)
Sophie Fedorovitch 1893–1953 (London, 1955) [Catalogue of 'A Memorial Exhibition of Designs for Ballet, Opera and Stage' at the Victoria and Albert Museum from 8 December 1955–January 1956 and then at a number of centres in England and Scotland during 1956]

Jackson, Sir Barry see Sheringham, George and Morrison B.

Jenkins, David Fraser, *et al.*
John Piper (London, 1983) [Catalogue of exhibition at the Tate Gallery 30 November 1983–22 January 1984]

Kochno, Boris
Christian Bérard (Paris, 1987)

Koltai, Ralph
'Theatre Design – The Exploration of Space', *Journal of the Royal Society of Arts*, no. 5368 vol. 135, (London, March 1987), pp. 298–309

Komisarjevsky, Theodore and Simonson, Lee
'Settings & Costumes of the Modern Stage', *The Studio* Winter Number (London, 1933)

Komisarjevsky, Theodore
''Dekoratzia' v sovremennom teatre' ['Decoration' in the contemporary theatre'], *Maski* no. 3, (St Petersburg, 1913–14), pp. 20–39

Laver, James
'The Russian Ballet: A retrospect – 1', *The Studio* vol. 93 no. 410, (London, May 1927), pp. 307–11

Laver, James
'The French Theatre', *The Studio* vol. 120 no. 569 (London, August 1940), pp. 52–9

Laver, James
Drama, its costume and décor (London, 1951)

Laver, James (introduction)
Mstislav V. Dobujinsky, 'Memorial Exhibition' at the Victoria and Albert Museum [catalogue] (London, 1959)

Laver, James
Costume in the theatre (London, 1964)

Levinson, André
'L'Esthétique de la Revue de Music-Hall – Un Vent de Folie', *L'Art Vivant* 15 April 1927, (Paris), p. 289

Levinson, André
'Revues à Grand Spectacle', *L'Art Vivant* 15 January 1928, (Paris), pp. 63–4

Levinson, André
'Décors', *L'Art Vivant* 15 December 1928, (Paris), pp. 971–2

Lindsay, Jack
Paintings and Drawings by Leslie Hurry (London, 1950)

MacInnes, Colin
Great Bardfield Artists (Ipswich *c.*1960)

McGowan, Margaret M.
The Court Ballet of Louis XIII (London, 1987)

Melvin, Duncan (editor)
Souvenirs de Ballet (London, 1949)

Moussinac, Léon
La décoration théâtrale (Paris, 1922)

Nagler, A. M.
A Source Book in Theatrical History (New York, 1952)

Nash, George
Edward Gordon Craig 1872–1966 (London, 1967, amended 1971)
[Catalogue of an exhibition at the Victoria and Albert Museum]

Nuzzi, Cristina
Umberto Brunelleschi, illustrazione, moda e teatro (1879–1949) (Milan, 1979)

Osborne, John
The Meiningen Court Theatre 1866–1890 (Cambridge, England, 1988)

Parnack, Valentin
Gontcharova Larionow – L'Art Décoratif Théâtral Moderne (Paris, 1919)

Polunin, Vladimir
The Continental Method of Scene Painting (London, 1927)

Rambert, Marie
Quicksilver (London, 1972)

Reade, Brian
Ballet Designs and Illustrations, 1581–1940 (London, 1967)
[a catalogue raisonné of designs and illustrations in the Victoria and Albert Museum]

Rischbieter, Henning (editor)
Art and the Stage in the 20th century (Greenwich, Connecticut, 1969)

Robertson, Bryan; Sonnabend, Yolanda; Crisp, Clement
Yolanda Sonnabend – Stage designs and Paintings (London, 1985)
[catalogue of an exhibition at the Serpentine Gallery, London, 30 November 1985–5 January 1986]

Roose-Evans, James
Directing a Play (London, 1968)

Roose-Evans, James
Experimental Theatre (London, revised edition 1984)

Rosenfeld, Sybil
A Short History of Scene Design in Great Britain (Oxford, 1973)

Rouché, Jacques
L'Art théâtral moderne (Paris, 1910, reissued 1924)

Salmina-Haskell, Larissa
Russian drawings in the Victoria and Albert Museum (London, 1972)

Schouvaloff, Alexander
Set and costume designs for ballet and theatre, Catalogue of the Thyssen-Bornemisza Collection (London, 1987)

Schouvaloff, Alexander and Borovsky, Victor
Stravinsky on Stage (London, 1982)

Scize, Pierre
'La Classe du Théâtre', *Art et Décoration* vol. xlviii (Paris, 1925) pp.193–204

Sheringham, George and Laver, James
Design in the Theatre (London, 1927)

Sheringham, George and Morrison, B.
Robes of Thespis, Costume design by modern artists (London, 1928)

Simonson, Lee
The stage is set (New York, 1932)

Simonson, Lee
The designer in the theatre, [introduction to exhibition catalogue] Theatre Art, Museum of Modern Art (New York, 1934)

Simonson, Lee
The Art of Scenic Design (New York, 1950)

Sonrel, Pierre
Traité de Scénographie (Paris, 1943, reissued 1984)

Stanislavsky, Constantin
My Life in Art (London, 1924)

Steinberg, Cobbett (editor)
The Dance Anthology (New York, 1980)

Strong, Roy; Guest, Ivor; Buckle, Richard
Designing for the Dancer (London, 1981)

Strong, Roy
Art and Power (Woodbridge, Suffolk, 1984)

Svetlow, Valérien
'Les peintres décorateurs russes', *Comoedia Illustré* no. 17, (Paris, 5 June 1913)

Watkins, Ronald
On Producing Shakespeare (London, 1950)

Wenger, John
American Stage Designs, (New York, 1919) [Catalogue]

Whitworth, Geoffrey
Theatre in Action (London, 1938)

Biographical index of designers

Numbers refer to catalogue numbers

Anderson, Percy (1851–1928), 70
English designer associated with the D'Oyly Carte company and His Majesty's Theatre, including designs for Oscar Ashe's production of *Chu Chin Chow* (1916) which ran for a record-making 2,238 perfomances

Anonymous, 78a, b, c

Arrighi, Luciana (born 1942), 73
Born in Rio de Janeiro of Italian father and Australian mother. Painter, stage and film designer. Work includes costumes for operas, plays and, especially, films. Television work with Ken Russell *Isadora, Rousseau, Rosetti*. Films include *Women in Love, My Brilliant Career*. Designed musical *I and Albert*, opera *Cataline* for Scottish Opera. *School for Scandal* National Theatre 1990.

Bailey, James (1922–80), 20, 29
English painter and designer associated with Sadler's Wells ballet, operas for Covent Garden and a number of productions for the Shakespeare Memorial Theatre, Stratford-upon-Avon

Bakst, Léon (1866–1924), 55, 65, 74
Russian painter, illustrator and theatre designer. Real name Lev Samoilovitch Rosenberg. One of the co-founders (with Alexandre Benois [see below] and others) of the *World of Art* group which led to formation of the Ballets Russes. Revolutionized theatre design with *Schéhérazade* (1910). Lived mostly in Paris after 1910. Designed many productions for Diaghilev until final quarrel after *The Sleeping Princess* (1921). Also closely associated with gala productions of Ida Rubinstein

Benois, Alexandre (1870–1960), 10, 33, 54
Russian painter, theatre designer, writer, critic and art historian. Co-founder and 'artistic director' of Ballets Russes for which he designed several productions including *Petrushka*.

Berain, Jean *the elder* (1640–1711), 9
Some references say born 1637. Trained under and succeeded Henri Gissey (1621–1673) as the *Dessinateur de la Chambre et du Cabinet du Roi*. From 1675 responsible for costumes and scenery for carnivals and fêtes, decorations for carousels, funerals and firework displays. Theatre work after 1681 mainly for the Opéra, Paris and therefore marked transition between *ballet de cour* and public theatre

Bérard, Christian (1902–49), 62
French painter and designer. Worked chiefly with Boris Kochno on ballets including *Cotillon* (1932) for Ballet Russe de Monte Carlo, *Les Forains* (1945) for Ballets des Champs-Elysées, and with Louis Jouvet on plays especially productions of Molière

Bibiena *see* Galli

Björnson, Maria (born 1949), 79a, b
Born in Paris of Norwegian and Rumanian parents but brought up in England. Began at Glasgow Citizens' Theatre. Royal Shakespeare Company (including *The Tempest, Hamlet* (1985). Much of her work is for opera including *The Magic Flute, Seraglio* for Scottish Opera, *Toussaint* for English National Opera, *The Makropoulos Case, Ernani* for Welsh National Opera and companies in Germany, Ireland, Australia and the United States. Lately associated with Andrew Lloyd Webber, *Phantom of the Opera* (1986), *Aspects of Love* (1989)

Boquet, Louis René (studio of) (1717–1814), 59
Pupil of François Boucher, succeeded Jean-Baptiste Martin (1659–1735) as chief designer at the Opéra, Paris in 1760. Also responsible for costumes for court entertainments at Versailles and elsewhere until 1782

Brunelleschi, Umberto (1879–1949), 44
Italian painter, fashion designer, illustrator and theatre designer principally of costumes for French revue including Folies Bergère, Mogador and Marigny theatres, Paris and costumes for operas at La Scala, Milan and Maggio Musicale, Florence including *Turandot* (1940)

Burra, Edward (1905–76), 5
English painter and occasional designer for the theatre, especially ballet. First work for the theatre *Rio Grande* (1931). Major productions include Robert Helpmann's *Miracle in the Gorbals* (1944) and Frederick Ashton's *Don Juan* (1948) for Sadler's Wells ballet

Bury, John (born 1925), 34
English designer. Began at Joan Littlewood's Theatre Workshop at Theatre Royal, Stratford East, London, resident designer 1954–1964. Head of Design for Royal Shakespeare Company 1964–1973. Head of design at National Theatre from 1973. Particularly associated with Peter Hall. Gold medal, Prague Quadriennale, 1975

Calthrop, Gladys (*c*.1900–80), 23
Particularly associated with Noël Coward for whom she designed most of the first productions of his plays and other works for the theatre including *The Vortex* (1924), *Hay Fever* (1925), *Private Lives* (1930), *Bitter Sweet* and *Cavalcade* (1931), *Design for Living* (1932) and film *In Which We Serve* (1944)

Caney, Robert (1847–1911), 21
Active during the last quarter of the nineteenth century, particularly on sets for the spectacular Christmas pantomimes at Theatre Royal, Drury Lane

Chappell, William (born 1909), 63
English dancer (first appearance 1929), choreographer of ballets and musicals. Director of revues: *Lyric Revue* (1951), *Globe Revue* (1952), *High Spirits* (1953). Designer of ballets for Camargo Society from 1932 and for Sadler's Wells ballet, notably *Giselle* and *Les Rendezvous* (1934), *Les Patineurs* (1937). Since 1955 chiefly director of plays

Chitty, Alison (born 1948), 13
English designer. Assistant Designer at Victoria Theatre, Stoke-on-Trent 1971–74, Head of Design 1974–77. Productions at Theatre Royal, Stratford East, *Old King Cole*, for Riverside Studios, Royal Shakespeare Company (including *Tartuffe, Volpone*), Crucible Theatre, Sheffield. Resident designer at National Theatre (including *A Month in the Country, Don Juan, Danton's Death, Tales from Hollywood*). For Peter Hall *Orpheus Descending* (1988)

Clavé, Antoni (born 1913), 90
Spanish painter, graphic artist and sculptor. Born in Barcelona but working mainly in France. In theatre designed mostly ballets: *Los Caprichos* (1946), and worked mostly with choreographer Roland Petit on ballets including *Carmen* (1949), *Ballabile* (1950), *Deuil en 24 heures* (1953)

Comelli, Attilio (*c*.1858–1925), 41
There were two brothers Comelli, Attilio and E(?). Both regularly employed as costume designers for extravagant entertainments at Alhambra, Drury

Lane and other London theatres at the end of the nineteenth and beginning of the twentieth centuries

Craig, Edward Gordon (1872–1966), 47
English actor, director, designer, writer and above all theorist and 'philosopher' of the theatre whose influence, through his ideas and his writing, endures wherever theatre is practised

Crage, Basil (active 1890s), 40a, b, c
Nothing is known of this artist except that he too, as a contemporary of the Comelli brothers above, must have been employed as costume designer for variety entertainments

Cruddas, Audrey (1914–79), 66a, b, c, d
Born in Johannesburg, came to England at an early age. First theatre work – costumes for *The White Devil* (1947). Sets and costumes for Shakespeare Memorial Theatre, Stratford-upon-Avon, Old Vic Theatre, *Aida* for Royal Opera House, Covent Garden, and *Antony and Cleopatra* and *Caesar and Cleopatra* for Laurence Olivier and Vivien Leigh for which she won American Donaldson Award, 1951–2 season

Dany, L. (active 1930s), 43
French designer. Work includes costumes and sets for Parisian revues at Concert Mayol and Folies Bergère including *Nuits de Folies* (1932–3), *Folies en Folie* (1934–5), *Femmes en Folie* (1936–6)

de Chirico, Giorgio (1888–1978), 58
Italian painter born in Greece. First work for the theatre *Giara* (1924) for Ballets Suédois. *Le Bal* for Diaghilev his most celebrated work. Other ballets include *Pulcinella* (1930) for Russian Opera in Paris, *Protée* (1938) for Colonel de Basil's Ballets Russes. Later theatre work *The Legend of Joseph* (1951) for La Scala, Milan and *Don Quixote* (1953) for Maggio Musicale, Florence

de Loutherbourg, Philippe Jacques (1740–1812), 18a, b, c
Alsatian painter who came to London in 1771. Engaged by David Garrick, actor-manager of Drury Lane, to be scenic director. Responsible for number of technical innovations in scenery, lighting and sound effects. Introduced degree of naturalism into the theatre which led to development of realism and historical accuracy

Dobujinsky, Mstislav (1875–1957), 31, 75
Russian painter, book illustrator and member of *Mir Iskusstvo* (*The World of Art*) group. First theatre work for Meyerhold in 1907. Worked for Moscow Art Theatre including *A Month in the Country* (1909), and for Diaghilev's Ballets Russes *Midas* (1914). Left Russia in 1924, settled in Lithuania but also worked in England. Joined Michael Chekhov's theatre in New York, 1939. Also designed for Metropolitan Opera, City Center Opera, Ballet Theatre, International Ballet Company and other American and Canadian companies

Erté (Romain de Tirtoff) (born 1892), 42
Russian designer, fashion designer, illustrator and sculptor. Pseudonymn is French pronunciation of the initial letters of his Russian name. Went to Paris in 1912. 1913 designer for couturier Paul Poiret. Exclusive ten-year contract with *Harper's Bazar* (1916–26) then renewed for further ten years. Regularly designed sets and costumes for Folies Bergère (1919–1936) and other revues in Paris (Le Lido 1941–46), London, Blackpool (1947–52 and 1955–1959), and New York. Sets and costumes for operas including *Der Rosenkavalier* (1980) for Glyndebourne

Exter, Alexandra (1882–1949), 49
Russian painter, theatre and film designer, marionette maker. Studied in Paris. Friend of Picasso, Braque, Apollinaire and Marinetti. First theatre work 'cubist' designs for *Famira Kifared* at Kamerny (Chamber) Theatre, Moscow (1916), also *Romeo and Juliet* (1921). Left Russia 1924. Sets and costumes for film *Aelita* (1924). Subsequently many unidentified projects. Died in France in obscurity

Fedorovitch, Sophie (1893–1953), 6, 61a, b
Russian painter. Settled in London 1920. Lifelong friendship with choreographer Frederick Ashton whom she met through Marie Rambert. Early theatre work ballets for Ballet Club and Sadler's Wells including *Horoscope* (1938), *Dante Sonata* (1940), *La Fête Etrange* (1940) and *Symphonic Variations* (1946). Also designed operas, notably *La Traviata* (1948) and *Madama Butterfly* (1950) for Covent Garden and plays, notably *The Winter's Tale* (1951) for John Gielgud

Fraser, Claude Lovat (1890–1921), 30, 52
English designer and book-illustrator. Major work for theatre for actor-manager Nigel Playfair and Lyric Theatre, Hammersmith, *As You Like It* (1919, Stratford-upon-Avon revived 1920, Hammersmith), *The Beggar's Opera* (1920), and ballet *Nursery Rhymes* (1921) for Tamara Karsavina

Furse, Roger (1903–72), 15, 26
English painter and designer. As well as ballets, *The Prospect Before Us* (1940) and *Adam Zero* (1946) for Sadler's Wells, designed plays and films. Especially associated with Laurence Olivier on plays *Venus Observed*, *Caesar and Cleopatra*, *Antony and Cleopatra*, *The Sleeping Prince* and films *Hamlet*, *Richard III*. Also worked at Shakespeare Memorial Theatre, Stratford-upon-Avon, *Macbeth* (1955)

Galli, Ferdinando da Bibiena (1657–1743), 2, 16
Father of family of scenic artists and architects who worked in all major European theatres in baroque style. Began by working for Duke of Parma at Teatro Farnese. Subsequently moved to Vienna at command of Emperor Charles VI and worked with brother Francesco. Sons and grandson continued family tradition. Often impossible to differentiate their drawings

Gesmar, Charles (1900–1928), 45
French graphic artist, poster and theatre designer. Worked in Paris in the 1920s. Costumes for music-hall revues especially for the star Mistinguett

Goffin, Peter (1906–1974), 69, 72
English interior decorator, mural painter and designer. Resident director and later designer at Barn Theatre, Chesham Bois 1935–36. Designer for D'Oyly Carte Opera Company 1949–61, subsequently Artistic Director

Gontcharova, Natalia (1881–1962), 12
Russian painter and designer. Lived with Larionov (see below) from 1903; they married in 1955. Both left Russia in 1915. Lived in Paris. Major productions for Diaghilev's Ballets Russes were *Le Coq d'Or* (1914), *Les Noces d'Aurore* (1922), *Les Noces* (1923), *Nuit sur le Mont Chauve* (1923) and revival of *The Firebird* (1926) which she re-created for Sadler's Wells ballet in 1954. Other theatre work, opera and ballet, in Paris, Monte Carlo and London

Grieve, Thomas (1799–1882), 19
English scene-painter. Elder son of John Henderson and member of family of scenic artists. Worked between Covent Garden and Drury Lane. First at Covent Garden, then Drury Lane 1835–39, then principal painter at Covent Garden under Madame Vestris's and her husband, Charles Matthews', management 1839–42, then again Drury Lane and for Charles Kean at Princess's

Gris, Juan (1887–1927), 57
Spanish painter. Moved to Paris in 1906, lived in same house as Picasso. In addition to costume for *Daphnis and Chloé* designed ballet *La Tentation de la Bergère* and operas *La Colombe*, *L'Education Manquée* and *Les Dieux Mendiants* for Diaghilev's Ballets Russes. In 1924 also designed and managed *Fête merveilleuse* in the Hall of Mirrors at Versailles

Hardy, Dudley (1866–1922), 82
English poster artist active end of nineteenth beginning of twentieth centuries

Harris, George W. (1878–1929), 22
English painter, etcher and designer. Invented new techniques of scene painting. Particularly associated with Basil Dean productions. Important productions include Galsworthy's *The Forest*, *R.U.R.*, *Fifinella* (1920), *Will Shakespeare* (1921)

Hepworth, Dame Barbara (1903–75), 86
British sculptor. Carved in stone, introduced 'hole' in 1931 and, by 1934, concentrated on abstract sculpture and in 1938 began to stretch strings across hole or cavity. From 1939 lived in St Ives, Cornwall, and postwar sculpture no longer 'austerely abstract'. Her home now an outstation of the Tate Gallery

Herbert, Jocelyn (born 1917), 39
English theatre and film designer. Major theatre work, 30 new productions, for English Stage Company at Royal Court Theatre beginning with *The Chairs* (1957). Work also includes Royal Shakespeare Company *Richard III* (1961), National Theatre *Othello* (1964) and *The Oresteia* (1981) and operas including Sadler's Wells *Orpheus and Euridice* (1966), Paris Opéra *La Forza del Destino* (1975) and Metropolitan New York *Lulu* (1977). Films include *Hamlet, Isadora, If . . .*

Heslewood, Tom (1868–1959), 38
English actor and costume designer. First appearance in 1892 at Criterion in *Haste to the Wedding*. Associated with Lewis Waller 1898–1915. Costume designs include *A Lady of Quality* (1899), *Bonnie Dundee* (1900), *Queen's Romance* (1903), *His Majesty's Servant* (1904), *Hamlet* (1905) for H. B. Irving, also in business as stage costumier 1914–29.

Hockney, David (born 1937), 85
English painter. First theatre work *Ubu Roi* (1966) Royal Court Theatre. Later work for Glyndebourne opera *The Rake's Progress* (1975), *The Magic Flute* (1978), for Metropolitan Opera House, New York two triple bills *Parade, Les Mamelles de Tirésias* and *L'Enfant et les Sortilèges* (1981), and Stravinsky's *Le Sacre du Printemps, Le Rossignol* and *Oedipus Rex* (1981), and San Francisco *Tristan und Isolde* (1987)

Hurry, Leslie (1909–78), 3, 51
English painter and designer. Discovered by Robert Helpmann for whom first theatre work, ballet *Hamlet* (1942). Also *Le Lac des Cygnes* (1943 revised 1952) for Sadler's Wells ballet. *Der Ring des Nibelungen* (1954) for Covent Garden. Regularly designed plays for Old Vic and Stratford-upon-Avon 1944–1963, and Stratford Ontario 1964–73

Irving, Laurence, CBE (1897–1988), 11
English painter, illustrator, theatre and film designer, writer and biographer of his grandfather Sir Henry Irving, and inspirer of Theatre Museum. Art director in Hollywood to Douglas Fairbanks for *The Man in the Iron Mask* (1928) and *The Taming of the Shrew* (1929). Plays include *The Circle, The Painted Veil* (1931), *Clive of India* (1934), *Murder in the Cathedral* (1935), *Hamlet* at Old Vic (1950), *Man and Superman* (1951), *Pygmalion* (1953), *The Wild Duck* (1975), *The Broken Jug* (1958)

Koltai, Ralph, CBE (born 1924), 50
Hungarian-German descent. Designed over 180 productions of opera, drama, dance in Europe, United States and Australia. Major work in England, Associate Designer, Royal Shakespeare Company 1963–66 and from 1976 (over 25 productions), National Theatre, Royal Opera House *Taverner* (1972), *The Icebreak* (1977), English National Opera *The Ring Cycle* (1970–81). Directed and designed *The Flying Dutchman*, Hong Kong (1987). *Metropolis* (1988). Gold medal. Prague Quadriennale, 1975

Lancaster, Sir Osbert (1908–86), 7
English cartoonist, writer on architecture, painter and theatre designer. Main work for ballet, John Cranko's *Pineapple Poll* (1951) and *Bonne Bouche* (1952), *Coppélia* (1954), *La Fille Mal Gardée* (1960) and for Glyndebourne opera including *The Rake's Progress* (1953)

Larionov, Michel (1881–1964), 89
Russian painter, invented 'rayonnism' 1909. (See Gontcharova above.) Work for Diaghilev's Ballets Russes *Soleil de Nuit* (1915) *Contes Russes* (1916–19), *Chout* (1921) and *Renard* (1922 revived 1929)

Meninsky, Bernard (1891–1950), 91
British painter, draughtsman. Born in Ukraine, brought to England when six weeks old. Joined Edward Gordon Craig's school in Florence (1913)

teacher of drawing and stage design. 1914–18 official war artist. Ballets for Markova-Dolin company

Moiseiwitsch, Tanya, CBE (born 1914), 53
Born in London. First production *The Faithful* (1934). Abbey Theatre, Dublin 1935–39, weekly repertory at Oxford Playhouse 1941–44, Playhouse, Liverpool 1944–45. Productions at Old Vic, Sadler's Wells, Memorial Theatre, Stratford-upon-Avon. Designed Festival Tent, Stratford, Ontario 1953 with Tyrone Guthrie and over 20 productions for annual festivals. Associate Director, Stratford Festival. Also productions at Tyrone Guthrie Theatre, Minneapolis 1963–65.

Nash, Paul (1889–1946), 60a, b
English painter, book illustrator, textile designer and occasional theatre designer. In tradition of English landscape painting with poetic character and sense of place. Official war artist 1917 and during Second World War. Designs for *A Midsummer Night's Dream* and *King Lear* in Player's Shakespeare Series, edited by Granville Barker.

Norris, Herbert (died 1950), 68
English designer active during first quarter of twentieth century

Parigi, Giulio (1571–1635), 1
Italian theatre designer. Some references give date of birth as 1580. Pupil and successor of Bernardo Buontalenti (1536–1608) at the Medici Court in Florence. Succeeded in turn by son Alfonso

Pemberton, Reece (1914–77), 17a, b, c, d, 25
English designer for films, theatre and television. Major London productions include *Waters of the Moon* (1951), *Marching Song* (1954), *The Chalk Garden* (1966), *The Winslow Boy* (1970). Often associated with productions by Frith Banbury. Lectured on design Bristol University 1969–71

Picasso, Pablo (1881–1973), 56a, b, c
Spanish but lived and worked for the most part in France. After *Parade* (1917) designed three more ballets for Diaghilev and the Ballets Russes – *Le Tricorne* (1919), *Pulcinella* (1920) and *Cuadro Flamenco* (1921), and front cloth for *Le Train Bleu* (1924). Also ballet *Mercure* (1924) for Les Soirées de Paris and drop-curtain for *Le Rendez-vous* (1946) for Ballets des Champs Elysées, and for Serge Lifar backcloth for *L'Après-Midi d'un Faune* (1962, not used until 1965) and *Icare* (1962)

Piper, John, C. H. (born 1903), 14, 81a, b, c, d
English painter, writer and illustrator, also work in stained glass and tapestry. First theatre work abstract design for Stephen Spender's *Trial of a Judge* (1938) for Group Theatre. Front cloth for William Walton's *Façade* (1942). Long association with Glyndebourne, the Royal Opera House, Covent Garden and especially the operas of Benjamin Britten *The Rape of Lucretia* (1946), *Albert Herring* (1947), *Billy Budd* (1951), *The Turn of the Screw* (1954), *A Midsummer Night's Dream* (1960), *Owen Wyngrave* (1970) and *Death in Venice* (1973)

Pocock, Isaac (1782–1835), 77a, b
English painter and dramatist. Author of several popular melodramas, including *The Miller and his Men* (1813), and adaptations from Walter Scott produced at Covent Garden and Drury Lane

Rabel, Daniel (active 1613–34), 8, 27, 36, 37, 46
French costume designer. Trained as a painter. Sent to Madrid 1616 to paint portrait of Anne of Austria. First recorded receiving 100 livres for designing costumes for *Le Ballet de Tancrède* (1619), for which Tommaso Francini designed scenery

Richards, Ceri (1903–71), 87
Welsh painter. As well as paintings, made relief constructions, drawings, prints, book illustrations, and mural decorations for ships of Orient Line (1937). Also designed Benjamin Britten's *Noyes Fludde* (1958) for Aldeburgh

Ricketts, Charles (1866–1931) (*see* also Goffin, Peter 69), 71
English costume designer who led the way against unimaginative realism.

Attracted particular attention with designs for George Bernard Shaw's *Saint Joan* (1923)

Schervashidze, Prince Alexandre (1869–1968) 80a, b
Russian designer and scene painter associated with Diaghilev and the Ballets Russes. Lived in France after the revolution. Painted famous front cloth for *Le Train Bleu* (1924) designed by Picasso who signed and dedicated it to Diaghilev

Schwabe, Randolph (1885–1948), 35
Painter, illustrator and costume designer. *Romeo and Juliet, The Enchanted Cottage*. Illustrated Cyril Beaumont's *The Sleeping Princess* for 'Impressions of the Russian Ballet' series (1921)

Scott, J. Hutchinson (1924–77), 24
English theatre designer. Resident designer at Oxford Playhouse 1945–48, Bristol Old Vic 1949–53. London productions from 1951. Perfected the art of designing scenery for drawing-room comedies including *Boeing-Boeing* (1962) and *No Sex Please – We're British* (1971). Designs for Old Vic and Shakespeare Memorial Theatre. Founder member of Crest Theatre, Toronto

Searle, Ronald (born 1920), 84
English painter, cartoonist, humourist, satirist and writer. Created the Schoolgirls of St Trinians 1941 (abandoned them 1953). Five films based on the characters. *Punch* theatre artist 1949–62. Designed films including *John Gilpin* (1951), *On the Twelfth Day* (1954) and animated sequence in *Those Magnificent Men in Their Flying Machines* (1965)

Sheringham, George (1884–1937), 32
English painter and theatre designer. Productions include *Midsummer Madness* (1924), *The Duenna* (1924) and new designs for Gilbert and Sullivan operas *The Pirates of Penzance, HMS. Pinafore, Patience* (1919). Also *Twelfth Night* at Stratford-upon-Avon (1932)

Sonnabend, Yolanda (born 1935), 64
Painter and designer. Born in Rhodesia, resident in England since 1954. Among plays designed *Phèdre* (1966), *The Tempest* (1968), *Othello* (1970) directed by Frank Hauser at Oxford Playhouse, among operas *The Turn of the Screw* (1971 and 72) at Aldeburgh Festival. Particularly associated with choreographer Kenneth MacMillan and ballets *Symphony* (1963 and 75), *Rituals* (1975), *Requiem* (1976), *Gloriana* (1977), *My Brother, My Sisters* (1978 and 80), *Playground* (1980), *Valley of Shadows* (1983) and *Different Drummer* (1984)

Stanfield, Clarkson (1794–1867), 28
English painter and scenic artist. Worked at Theatre Royal, Edinburgh 1831. Returned to London and was scenic director at Coburg and, later, at Theatre Royal, Drury Lane. Exhibited with success at Royal Academy in 1834 and did no more scene painting except for two productions for Macready in 1837 and 1842 and for private production by Charles Dickens of *The Frozen Deep*. Last theatrical work for Adelphi in 1858

Stern, Ernst (1876–1954), 48
German theatre designer born in Rumania, trained in Munich. 1906 art director to Max Reinhardt's theatres. Associated with Reinhardt until 1921 on productions including *The Miracle* (1912) and plays by Shakespeare, Strindberg, Ibsen, Tolstoy. Also operas *La Belle Hélène* and *Orphée aux Enfers*. After 1921 designed films for Ernst Lubitsch, revivals of *The Merry Widow, The Three Musketeers* and original production of *The White Horse Inn. King Lear* (1943) for Donald Wolfit

Tchelitchew, Pavel (1898–1957), 83
Russian painter. Fled to Kiev 1918, to Berlin 1921, went to Paris 1923, United States 1934. Became American citizen 1952. Designed *Ode* (1928) for Diaghilev's Ballets Russes, *Errante* (1933) and *Balustrade* (1941) for Balanchine, *Nobilissima Visione* (1938) for Massine

Ter-Arutunian, Rouben (born 1920), 88
Born in Tiflis, educated in Berlin, Vienna, Paris. Designer of operas, musicals, ballets, plays and for television. First production *The Bartered Bride* (1941) in Dresden. In USA from 1951. Associated with American Shakespeare Festival Theatre at Stratford Connecticut 1956–57, designed new permanent stage there 1960, Martha Graham since 1961. Also associated with New York City Ballet, designs include *Swan Lake* (1952), *The Nutcracker* (1964), *Ballet Imperial* (1964), *The Song of the Nightingale* (1972). For The Royal Ballet *Laborintus* (1972)

Thomas, Théophile (c.1846–1916), 76
French costumier working in the last quarter of nineteenth century

Utrillo, Maurice (1883–1955) (*see* Schervashidze, Prince Alexandre 80a and b)
French painter. Natural son of Suzanne Valadon. No formal training, but persuaded by Diaghilev to work for the theatre, *Barabau* (1925)

Wakhevitch, Georges (1907–84), 4
Russian theatre and film designer. Settled in France in 1920s. Long collaboration with Cocteau on stage and screen with *L'Eternel Retour, L'Aigle à deux têtes, Le Jeune Homme et la Mort*. Also worked with Renoir on *Madame Bovary* and with Carné on *Les Visiteurs du Soir*. Worked with Peter Brook on plays e.g. *King Lear* and operas at Covent Garden *Boris Godunov* (1949), *The Tales of Hoffman* (1954) and *Otello* (1955)

Wilhelm (1858–1925), 67
Alias of William John Charles Pitcher. English costume designer, self-taught. First work at Theatre Royal, Drury Lane 1877, then at Alhambra 1878–1883 on ballets including *The Golden Wreath*, and Theatre Royal, Drury Lane pantomimes 1879–1897. Associated especially with ballets at Empire Theatre from 1887–1915 including, for Adeline Genée, *Old China* (1902), *High Jinks* (1904), *Cinderella* (1906) and *The Belle of the Ball* (1907). Continued to design for Genée after she left the Empire including *La Camargo* (1912) and *The Pretty Prentice* (1916)

Photographic acknowledgements

Designs are reproduced by kind permission of:

Mrs H. Rumbold for James Bailey
The Arnold Rood Collection for Edward Gordon Craig
Miss Mary Cheseldene for Audrey Cruddas
Mrs Michael Grimmer for Peter Goffin
Sir Alan Bowness for Dame Barbara Hepworth
John Armstrong for Leslie Hurry
Elizabeth, Lady Brunner and John Irving for Laurence Irving
Lady Lancaster for Sir Osbert Lancaster
Mrs Nora Meninsky for Bernard Meninsky
Mrs Rhiannon Gooding for Ceri Richards
Lady Barnes for Randolph Schwabe
Laurence Harbottle and John Duke for Jay Hutchinson Scott
Richard Nathanson for Pavel Tchelitchev
Paul Nash Trust for Paul Nash
Sevenarts London Ltd. for Erté

Photographs of all the designs are reproduced by arrangement with
the Board of Trustees, Victoria and Albert Museum, London

Every effort has been made to trace where necessary the copyright
owners of the designs. We regret and extend our sincere apologies
if there are any omissions in the acknowledgements, and would hope
to rectify them in a future edition

Index

The index is of names and titles in the introduction and catalogue entries. It excludes references under provenance, exhibitions and literature.

Abbey, Henry E. 193
Ackland, Rodney 74
Adam, Adolphe 64
Agustino, Bernardo 227
Agustino, Louis 227
Ainley, Henry 69
Albery Theatre *see* New Theatre
Aldeburgh Festival 30
Alhambra Theatre 142
Allen, Adrienne 70
Anderson, Clifton 102
Anderson, Percy 181
Andrews 196
Animated Tapestry, The 38
Anisfeld, Boris 140
Ansermet, Ernest 146
Apollinaire, Guillaume 30
Arnaud 119
Arnaud, Yvonne 72
Arrighi, Luciana 186
Arthurs, George 188
Ashton, Frederick 28, 156, 160
As You Like It 13, 130, 133, 136
Atys 37
Auget 120
Austin, Frederic 86

Babes in the Wood 110
Bailey, James 12, 13, 64, 84, 133
Baker, Mr 82
Bakst, Léon 9, 14, 140, 145, 148,
     165, 166, 188, on Picasso 146
Bal, Le 14, 150
Balanchine, George 140, 150, 204
Baldini, Mademoiselle 119
Ballet d'Apollon see Ballet du Roi
Ballet de la Debauche 80
Ballet de la Délivrance de Renaud 100
Ballet du Landy 80
Ballet du Roi 35
Ballet du Sérieux et du Grotesque 99
*Ballet Royal du Grand bal de la
     Douairière de Billbahaut* 120
Ballets de Monte Carlo 142
Ballets de Paris 230
Ballets Russes *see* Diaghilev's Ballets
     Russes
Banbury, Frith 54, 74
Barabau 133, 204
Barker, Ronnie 104
Barn Theatre, Singapore 216
Barrie, J. M. 154
Barrington, Rutland 174
Ba-Ta-Clan Theatre 112
Bataille, Gabriel 100
Bax, Arnold 154
Beaumont Cyril W. 134
Beckerley, John 216
Beggar's Opera, The 86
Belleville 100

Bellini, Vincenzo 82
Benois, Alexandre 12, 14, 38, 92,
     140, 142, 152
Benthall, Michael 22, 168
Berain, Jean -Louis 37
Bérard, Christian 14, 158
Bergsma, Deanne 163
Berkeley, Lennox 223
Berlin *see* theatres
Berlioz, Hector 158, 166
Bernhardt, Sarah 193
Bernstein, Aline 79
Bertram Mills' Great International
     Circus 15, 212
Besch, Anthony 186
Bibiena *see* Galli
Bibliothèque de l'Opéra, Paris 152
Bintley, David 163
Birtwistle, Harrison 94
Bizet, Georges 230
Björnson, Maria 15, 202
Blakely, Colin 104
Bliss, Arthur 136
Bluebell, Miss 114
Bluebell's Beautiful Ladies, Les 114
Boësset, Antoine 35, 99, 120
Boleslavsky, Richard 124
Bolm, Adolph 148
Boquet, Louis René 152
Bordier, René 99, 100, 120
Boussard 114
Braham, Leonora 174
Brandram, Rosina 181
Brannigan, Owen 139
Braque, Georges 140
Breasts of Tiresias, The 30
Brett, Jeremy 130
Bridgewater, Leslie 76
Britten, Benjamin 30, 46, 139
Brook, Peter 24
Brooke, Harry 110
Brown, Pamela 49
Brunelleschi, Umberto 13, 114, 116
Bull, John 97
Buonarotti, Michelangelo, the
     younger 18
Buontalenti, Bernardo 18
Burgess, John 202
Burra, Edward 12, 26
Burrill, Ena 76
Bury, John 94
Busch, Fritz 206

Cadell, Jean 74
Calthrop, Gladys 70
Caney, Robert 12, 66
Cantelo, April 223
Canut 119
Cape, Jonathan 163
Carmen 230

Cavaliers and Roundheads 82
Cecchetti, Enrico 92
Cellier, François 174, 181
Cenci, The 22
Cendrillon 12, 44
Chabelska, Marie 146
Chanel, Coco 156
Channon, Right Hon. Paul 220
Chant du Rossignol, Le 9
Chantrier 114, 119
Chappell, William 14, 160
Châtelet Theatre, Paris 38, 92, 145,
     146, 148
Chekhov, Anton 94
Cherry Orchard, The 94
Chitty, Alison 42
Christiné 114
Chronegk, Ludwig 51
Cibber, Colley 58
Cinderella and the Magic Soya Bean
     216
Clare, Mary 74
Clavé, Antoni 15, 230
Clifton, Miss 196
cloths, painted 133–9
Clunes, Alec 24
Coates, Edith 139
Cobb, Gladys 54
Cochran, Charles B. 33, 100
Cocteau, Jean 145, 146
Coleman, Basil 46
Coliseum *see* London Coliseum
Collins, Arthur 66, 110
Comelli, Attilio 66, 110
Comelli, E. 110
commedia dell'arte 218, 231
Cooke, Thomas Potter 196
Coombe, Mrs 196
Cooper, John 82
Coralli, Jean 64
costume (*see* Contents)
     ballet 140–163
     fantastical 13, 79
     historical 12, 33
     realistic 79
Covent Garden *see* Royal Opera
     House
Coward, Noël 70, 102
Crabbe, George 139
Crage, Basil 106
Craig, Edith 97
Craig, Edward Gordon 13, 124, 126
Cranko, John 30, 46, 222
Craven, Hawes 174, 181
Crawford, Mimi 40
Cross, Joan 46, 139
Cross, W. 66
Crozier, Eric 223
Crucible Theatre, Sheffield 11
Cruddas, Audrey 14, 165, 168

cubism 128, 146
Curran, Paul 130
Curti, Louis 198

Daisy, Amanda 119
Danco, Suzanne 206
Daniels, Ron 202
Danilova, Alexandra 150
Dany, L. 13, 114, 198
Daphnis and Chloé 14, 148
da Ponte, Lorenzo 206
da Vinci, Leonardo 211
Dean, Basil 69
Dear Charles 72
Death in Adagio 231
de Basil, Colonel, Ballets Russes 158
de Bear, Archibald
de Chirico, Giorgio 14, 140, 150
Decon, Claire Traverse 202
decor *see* scenery
de Courville, Albert P. 188
de Grand-Pré, César 120
Delaunay, Robert 140
de l'Estoile, Claude 120
Delius, Frederick 28, 69
de Loutherbourg, Philippe Jacques 58
de Luynes, Duc 35
de Madrazo, Federigo 145
Denny, W. H. 181
Derain, André 140
d'Erlanger, Frederic 44
Derval, Paul 114
Deshayes 114, 119
Desmond, Nigel 134
Desormière, Roger 204
de Tirtoff, Romain *see* Erté
Deutsches Theater, Berlin 126
de Valois, Ninette 26, 134, 140
de Viau, Théophile 35
de Zamora, José 119
Diaghilev, Serge 14, 141, 142, 211
Diaghilev's Ballets Russes 14, 15, 38, 140, 141, 148, 166, 204, 214, 227
diagonal perspective 20, 52
Diddear, Charles Bannister 82, 196
Dieu Bleu, Le 145
di Somi, Leone 33
Dobujinsky, Mstislav 15, 88, 188, 190
Dolin, Anton 148, 150
Don Giovanni 15, 206
Don Juan 128
Don Quixote 12, 26
Dove, Alfred 154
Dowell, Anthony 163
D'Oyly Carte, Dame Bridget 90
D'Oyly Carte, Rupert 178, 182
D'Oyly Carte Opera 14, 90, 173
Drottningholm 17
Drummond-Grant, Ann 184
Drury Lane *see* Theatre Royal, Drury Lane
Dukes, Ashley 156
Durand 119
Durand, Etienne 100

Eastwood, Thomas 24
Ebert, Carl 206
Efimov, Nicolas 227

Eggar, Samantha 104
Eglevsky, André 142
Elizabeth and Essex 46
Emden, Henry 66, 110
Enfants d'Edouard, Les 72
English Opera Group 223
Ermler, Mark 163
Erté (Romain de Tirtoff) 13, 112, 198
Evans, Edith 54
Evans, Geraint 206
Exchange Theatre, Manchester 11
Exter, Alexandra 13, 128, 146

Fedorovitch, Sophie 12, 28, 156
Femmes en Folie 13, 114
Filial Theatre 24
Finney, Albert 94
Five Flying Rixfords, The 212
Flecker, James Elroy 69
Florence 18
Fokine, Michel 38, 44, 69, 92, 145, 148, 163, 166
Folies Bergère 114, 116, 198
Fonteyn, Margot 26, 28, 64, 134, 160
Foster, Basil 154
Fragson, Harry 110
Francini, Tommaso 100, 120
Franklin 196
Franz, Ellen 51
Fraser, Claud Lovat 11–12, 13, 80, 86, 133, 136
Fréjol, Pierre 114
Freksa, Friedrich 124
Frères Plattier, Les 212
Froman, Marguerite 114
Furse, Roger 12, 13, 49, 76

Galli, Alessandro, da Bibiena 20
    Antonio, da Bibiena 20
    Carlo, da Bibiena 20
    Ferdinando, da Bibiena 20, 52
    Francesco, da Bibiena 20
    Giovanni Maria, da Bibiena 20
    Giuseppe, da Bibiena 20
Garrick, David 33, 58
Gautier, Emil 212
Gautier, Théophile 64, 166
Gavel 119
Gay, John 86
Georg II, Duke of Saxe-Meiningen 51
George, Marie 110
Gerdt, Pavel 38
Gerhard, Roberto 26
Gertrude Hoffmann Girls 119
Gesmar, Charles 13, 119, 198
Gielgud, John 74
Gilbert, W. S. 14, 90, 173–187
Gill, Peter 42
Gilpin, Sally 94
Giselle 12, 13, 64, 82, 133
Gismonda 15, 188, 193
Gitton, Jean 230
Giudizio di Paride, Il 18
Globe Theatre 11
Gloriana 12, 46
Glover, J. M. 66, 110
Gluck, Christoph Willibald 128

Glyndebourne Opera 206
Godfrey, Isidore 184, 186
Goffin, Peter 178, 184
Goldner, Charles 72
Gondoliers, The 14, 173, 180–187
Gontcharova, Natalia 12, 44, 140
Goossens, Eugene 86, 156
Gosset, Viviane 114
Gould, Diana 231
Goulding, Charles 178
Grant, Alexander 26
Grau, Maurice 193
Grieve, John Henderson 62
Grieve, Thomas 62
Grieve, Thomas Walford 62
Grieve, William 62
Griffin, Elsie 178
Griffith, Hugh 22
Gris, Juan 14, 140, 148
Grossmith, George 174
Guédron, Pierre 100
Guinness, Alec 49
Guitry, Lucien 193
Guthrie, Tyrone 139
Guy, Edmonde 119
Gwilym, Mike 202
Gyarmathy 114
Gzovska, Olga 124

Hahn, Reynaldo 145
Hale, Una 223
Halévy, Ludovic 230
Hall, Peter 94
Hamlet 9, 12, 24, 124
Hannen, Nicholas 49
Hardy, Dudley 15, 211, 212
Harris, George W. 69
Harrison, Kathleen 54
Harvey, Cynthia 163
Hassan 69
Hawtrey, Charles 102
Heine, Heinrich 64
Helpmann, Robert 26, 28, 134, 160
Hemsley, Thomas 223
Hepworth, Barbara 15, 222
Herbert, A. P. 156
Herbert, Jocelyn 15, 104
Hermite, Maurice 114
Hersey, David 94
Heslewood, Tom 102
Hierlinger, Adolph 227
Hiller, Wendy 54
Himmel, Chagrin 114
Hippodrome *see* London Hippodrome
Hirsch, Louis A. 188
His Majesty's Theatre 69
HMS Pinafore, or The Lass that loved a Sailor 90
Hockney, David 15, 211, 218, 221
Hoffmann, Gertrude 119
Hollaender, Victor 126
Hopkins, Anthony 130
Hôtel de Ville, Paris 120
Howes, Basil 40
Hoyer, Jean 227
Hullo, Tango! 188
Hunter, N. C. 54
Hurry, Leslie 13, 22, 133, 134

Imbert 120
Inghelbrecht, Désiré-Emile 145
Institute of Technology, New York 226
Invitation to the Waltz 166
Irving, Laurence 12, 33, 40
Ivanov, Lev 134, 163

Jack and the Beanstalk 12, 66
Jackson, Sir Barry 33
Jackson, Frederick 72
Jacobi, Derek 130
Jacques-Charles 119
Jeanmaire, Renée 230
Jeavons, Colin 104
Jefford, Barbara 22
Jerrold, Mary 74
Jones, Robert Edmond 10
Jubilee Hall, Aldeburgh 30
Judgement of Paris, The 18

Kachalov, Vasili 124
Kamerny Theatre, Moscow 128, 146
Karsavina, Tamara 92, 142, 145, 148, 154, 166
Kay, Charles 130
Kay, Richard 130
Kean, Charles 33, 62
Keane, Doris 97
Keen, Malcolm 69
Kellog, Shirley 188
Kikuta Troupe, The 212
King, Mr 82
King Arthur and the Knights of the Round Table 15, 196
King Lear 49
Knipper, Olga 124
Kochno, Boris 150
Koltai, Ralph 13, 123, 130
Kraus, Otakar 222
Kzewusky, Alec 119

Lac des Cygnes, Le 134
Lake, Molly 231
Lambert, Constant 26, 28, 64, 134, 160
Lambert, John 22
Lancaster, Osbert 12, 30
Lang, Robert 104
Lapotaire, Jane 42
Larionov, Michel 15, 140, 227
Laurençin, Marie 140
Laurent, Charles 119
Laver, James 128, 152
Laverdet 119
Lawrence, Gertrude 70
Lawson, Winifred 182
Leibovici 114
Leigh, Adele 222
Leigh, Vivien 76
Leighton, Margaret 49
Lely, Durward 174
Leno, Dan 66
Le Seyeux, Jean 114
Lester, Keith 231
Levy, Ethel 188
Lewis, Bertha 90, 182
Lewis, Richard 222
Lichine, David 44
Lifar, Serge 140, 141, 204, 227

Lincoln's Inn Fields 86
Lissanevitch, Boris 227
London *see* theatres
London Coliseum 154, 204
London Hippodrome 188
Longus 148
Lopokhova, Lydia 146
Louis XIII 35, 120
Louvre, Musée du, Paris 35, 99, 100, 120
Lully, Jean-Baptiste 37
Luzhski, Vasili 124
Lynch, Alfred 104
Lyric Theatre 97
Lyric Theatre, Hammersmith 74, 86, 136, 156
Lyttelton Theatre *see* National
Lytton, Henry A. 90, 178, 182

Macbeth 14, 33, 168
MacDonald, Murray 72
Mackerras, Charles 30, 223
Mackwood, John 216
Magnin, M. 193
Mamelles de Tirésias, Les 30
Marais 120
Maria Maddalena, Arch-Duchess of Austria 18
Mariinsky Theatre 38
Markova, Alicia 9, 231
Markova-Dolin Ballet 231
Marshall, Herbert 136
Mason, Brewster 42
Mason, Herbert 40
Mason, Ralph 186
Massalitinov, Nikolai 124
Massine, Leonide 141, 146, 158
Masterson, Valerie 186
Matisse, Henri 9, 140
May, Pamela 28
McCleery, R. 66, 110
McKellen, Ian 42
Medici, Cosimo 18
Meilhac, Henri 230
Meiningen Court Theatre 51
Melville, Alan 72
Melville, Winnie 90
Memorial Theatre *see* Shakespeare Memorial Theatre
Mendelson, Mira 88, 190
Ménestrier, Father Claude-François 37
Meninsky, Bernard 15, 231
Merimée, Prosper 230
Metropolis 15
Metropolitan Opera House, New York 88, 190, 218
Meyerbeer, Giacomo 160
Midsummer Marriage, The 222
Midsummer Night's Dream, A 15, 104, 202
Mieux que Nue! 13, 119
Mikado, The 14, 173, 174–179
Mills, Bertram 15, 212
Mills, Clifford 102
Mir Iskusstvo 14
Miró, Joan 140
Mistinguett 119
Moiseiwitsch, Tanya 13, 133, 139
Monroe, George W. 188

Monteux, Pierre 92
Moor, Decima 181
Moscow Art Theatre 24, 124
Moss Bros 76
Moulin Rouge Music-Hall 119
Mozart, Wolfgang Amadeus 206
Muldowney, Dominic 42, 94
Muller, Ingevelde 78

Nash, Paul 14, 154
Nathan, L. & H. 76
National Theatre 11, 42, 94, 130
Nells, Sylvia 86
Nemtchinova, Vera 142
Nesbitt, Cathleen 69
Neuville 114
New Theatre 49, 72, 74, 134
New Theatre, Oxford 231
Newton, Joy 134
New York *see* theatres
New York City Ballet 140
Nichols, E. 110
Nijinska, Bronislava 227
Nijinsky, Vaslav 38, 92, 142, 145, 148, 166
Nocturne 12, 28
Norris, Herbert 176
Northen, Michael 206

Octagon Theatre, Bolton 11
Ode 211
Oldham, Derek 90, 182
Old Ladies, The 13, 74
Old Mortality 82
Old Vic Company 49
Old Vic Theatre 22, 130, 168
Olivier, Laurence 15, 49, 70, 76
Olivier Theatre *see* National Theatre
Olympia, London 212
Opéra, Bibliothèque de l', Paris 152
Opéra, Monte Carlo 148, 150, 166
Opéra, Paris 140, 227
Orient Merveilleux ou 1002 Nuits de Bagdad, L' 13, 112
Orlando's Circus Horses 212
Orlov, Alexandre 92
Ornbo, Robert 130
Otway, Thomas 42
Owen, Reginald 102
Oyra, M. 119

Paddick, Hugh 42
Padilla, José 119
Palmer, Christine 186
Palmer, Mr. 196
Parade 14, 146, 218
Parigi, Giulio 12, 18
Paris *see* theatres
    Bibliothèque de l'Opéra 152
    Ballets de 230
Parker, Cecil 76
Parker, Louis N. 40
Parnaby, Bert 202
Passmore, Walter 110
Patineurs, Les 14, 160
Pavillon d'Armide, Le 12, 38
Pavlova, Anna 38
Pears, Peter 30, 46, 139, 223
Pemberton, Max 188
Pemberton, Reece 13, 52, 54, 74

Pennington, Michael 42
Pepusch, John Christopher 86
Percy, Esmé 69
periaktoi 18
Perkins, W. 66
Pernerstorfer, Alois 206
Perrault, Charles 44
perspective 17, 20
Peter Grimes 13, 133, 139
Petipa, Marius 134, 163
Petit, Roland 230
Petri, Mario 206
Petrushka 12, 92, 142
Phillips, John 22
Phoenix Theatre 24, 70, 76
Picasso, Pablo 14, 140, 146
Pickup, Ronald 130
Pierrot Luniare 221, 226
Piper, John 12, 15, 46, 206
Pitcher, William John Charles *see* Wilhelm
Platov, Marc 158
Plattier, Les Frères 212
Playfair, Nigel 80, 86, 136, 156
Plomer, William 46
Pocock, Isaac 15, 82, 196
Poel, William 126
Pollock, Anna 223
Polunin, Vladimir 204
Porter, Eric 168
Poulenc, Francis 30
Pounds, Courtice 181
Pratt, Peter 184
Princes Theatre 28, 178, 184, 230
Princess's Theatre 62
Pritchard, John 46, 222
Private Lives 70
Prokofiev, Serge 88, 190
proscenium 12, 17
Puritani, I 82

Quartermaine, Léon 69, 97
Quilter, Roger 102
Quinault, Philippe 37

Rabel, Daniel 35, 80, 99, 100, 120
Rambert, Marie 156
Ramsey, John 102
Ranalow, Frederick 86
Randall, André 114
Rankl, Karl 139
Rassine, Alexis 64
Ravel, Maurice 148
Rawsthorne, Alan 49
Rea, William J. 136
Read, John B. 130
Redgrave, Corin 104
Redgrave Lynn 104
Redman, Joyce 49
Reed, John 186
Reinhardt, Max 13, 126
Relph, George 49
Renaissance Theatre, Paris 193
Renard, Le 227
Rencher, Derek 163
Reynolds, Alfred 156
Riabouchinska, Tatiana 44
Richard 120
Richard III 58, 62
Richards, Ceri 15, 223

Richardson, Ralph 94
Richardson, Tony 104
Ricketts, Charles 173, 178, 182
Rieti, Vittorio 150, 202
Riverside Nights 156
Rixfords, Five Flying 212
Roberts, Alan 216
Roberts, J. H. 40
Roerich, Nicolas 140
Roger 119
Rogers, Paul 168
Romeo and Juliet 97
Ronsin 119
Round, Thomas 178, 184
Rose Theatre 11
Rosenfeld, Sybil 58, 126
Rosse, Herman 10, 165
Royal Ballet, The 140, 163
Royal Court Theatre 104
Royal Opera House 11, 26, 44, 46, 64, 139, 158, 163, 222
Royal Shakespeare Theatre 202
Rudd 114
Ruth 223

Sablon, Jean 114
Sackville-West, Edward 28
Sadler's Wells Ballet 26, 64, 134, 140
Sadler's Wells Theatre 139, 160
Sandford, Kenneth 184, 186
Sanger's, Elephants 212
Sarah Bernhardt Theatre, Paris 227
Sardanapalus 126
Sardou, Victorien 193
Sargent, Malcolm 90, 178, 182
Satie, Erik 146
Sauvajon, Marc-Gilbert 72
Saville Theatre 186
Savoy Theatre 90, 102, 174, 181, 182
Saxe-Meiningen, Duchy of 51
Saxe-Meiningen, Georg II, Duke of 51, 52
Scala Theatre 223
Scarlatti, Alessandro 231
scena par angolo 52
scene painting 204–5
scenery (*see* Contents)
    Baroque 52
    for Shakespeare 12
    historical 12
    optical illusion 12
    realistic 12, 51, 54
    symmetrical 12, 17, 52
    traditional 12
    two-dimensional 133–9
Schervashidze, Alexandre 15, 204
Schönberg, Arnold 226
Schwabe, Randolph 97
Scofield, Paul 24
Scott, Harold 54
Scott, J. Hutchinson 72
Scott, Walter 82
Scotto, Marc-César 119, 150
Searle, Ronald 15, 211, 216
Seltenhammer 114
Sergeyev, Nicholas 64, 134
Serov, Valentin 140
Seyler, Athene 136
Shaftesbury Theatre *see* Princes

247

Shakespeare Memorial Theatre 136
Shakespeare, William 11, 12, 24, 49,
    58, 62, 97, 104, 124, 130, 136,
    168, 202
Shakespeare's theatre 11
Shanks, Alec 198
Sheffield, Leo 90, 178, 182
Shelley, Percy Bysshe 22
Sheringham, George 90
Sillard 114
Simon, Moisès 114
Simonson, Lee 9–10, 51
Skin of Our Teeth, The 13, 76
Slater, Montague 139
Smith, Barry 202
Smith, Bruce 66, 110
Sokolova, Lydia 148, 204
Sologub, Vladimir 150
Song of the Nightingale, The 9
Sonnabend, Yolanda 14, 163
Spadaro 114
Spectre de la Rose, Le 14, 166
Spruce, Sally 76
Städtischen Bühnen, Cologne 128
Stanislavsky, Constantin 10, 124
Stanfield, Clarkson 82, 196
Starlight Express 15
Statkiewitz 146
Stephens, Robert 94, 130
Stern, Ernst 13, 126
Sterroll, Gertrude 154
Stevenson, Juliet 202
Strachey, Lytton 46
Stravinsky, Igor 92, 227
Sturgess, Arthur 66
Sullivan, Arthur 14, 90, 173–187
Sumurûn 126
Sutherland, Joan 222
Swan Lake 13, 14, 133, 134, 163
Sydney, Basil 97
Symphonie Fantastique 14, 158

Tairov, Alexander 13, 128, 146
Tales of the Arabian Nights 126
Tate, Harry 188
Taylor, Lily 76
Tchaikovsky, Piotr Ilyich 134, 163
Tchelitchew, Pavel 15, 211, 214
Tcherepnine, Nicolas 38, 166
telari 18
Ter-Arutunian, Rouben 15, 226
Terry, Ellen 97
Tetley, Glen 226
Theatre Royal, Drury Lane 58, 66,
    82, 110, 196
Theatre Royal, Haymarket 54
Theatres (in London unless
    otherwise stated):
    Albery see New
    Alhambra 142
    Barn, Singapore 216
    Ba-Ta-Clan, Paris 112
    Châtelet, Paris 38, 92, 145, 146,
        148
    Covent Garden see Royal Opera
        House
    Crucible, Sheffield 11
    Deutsches (Kammerspiele),
        Berlin 126

Drottningholm 17
Drury Lane see Theatre Royal,
    Drury Lane
Exchange, Manchester 11
Filial, Moscow 24
Folies Bergère, Paris 15, 114,
    116, 198
Globe 11
Glyndebourne, Sussex 206
His Majesty's 69
Hôtel de Ville, Paris 120
Institute of Technology, New
    York 226
Jubilee Hall, Aldeburgh 30
Kamerny, Moscow 128, 146
Lincoln's Inn Fields 86
London Coliseum 154, 204
London Hippodrome 188
Louvre, Paris 35, 99, 100, 120
Lyric 97
Lyric, Hammersmith 74, 86, 136,
    156
Lyttelton see National
Mariinsky, St Petersburg 38
Metropolitan, New York 88, 190,
    218
Moscow Art 24, 124
Moulin Rouge Music-Hall, Paris
    119
National 42, 94, 130
New 49, 72, 74, 134
New, Oxford 231
Octagon, Bolton 11
Olc Vic 22, 130, 168
Olympia 212
Opéra, Monte Carlo 148, 150,
    166
Opéra, Paris 140, 227
Phoenix 24, 70, 76
Princes 28, 178, 184, 230
Princess's 62
Renaissance, Paris 193
Rose 11
Royal Court 104
Royal Opera House 26, 44, 46,
    64, 139, 158, 163, 222
Royal Shakespeare, Stratford-
    upon-Avon 202
Sadler's Wells 139, 160
Sarah Bernhardt, Paris 227
Saville 186
Savoy 90, 102, 174, 181, 182
Scala, Milan 223
Shakespeare Memorial,
    Stratford-upon-Avon 136
Shaftesbury see Princes
Städtischen Bühnen, Cologne
    128
Theatre Royal, Drury Lane 58,
    66, 82, 110, 196
Theatre Royal, Haymarket 54
Uffizi, Florence 18
Vaudeville 40
Thomas, Théophile 15, 188, 193
Thorndike, Sybil 54
Thyl, Tom 119
Tiepolo, Giovanni Domenico 218
Tippett, Michael 222
Tiresias 12, 30

Todd, Ann 168
Toguri, David 202
Tolstoy, Leo 88, 190
Toumanova, Tamara 158
Toye, Jennifer 184
Tragedy of Fashion, A 156
Truth about the Russian Dancers,
    The 14, 154
Turleigh, Veronica 22
Tushingham, Rita 104
Tutin, Dorothy 94
tutu 152

Uffizi Palace 18
Ure, Mary 24
Utrillo, Maurice 15, 133, 204

Vandenhoff, John 82
Vaudeville Theatre 40
Vaudeville Vanities 40
Vaudoyer, Jean-Louis 166
Venetian Wedding, A 12, 40
Venice Preserv'd 42
Vernoy de Saint-Georges, Jules
    Henri 64
Vespucci, Amerigo 18
Vic-Wells Ballet 28, 160
Vining, Mrs 196
Vyvyan, Jennifer 30

Wakhevitch, Georges 12, 24
Wallace, Kevin 202
Walpole, Hugh 74
War and Peace 15, 88, 188, 190
Waters of the Moon 54
Weber, Carl-Maria von 166
Welbury, Robin 216
Wenger, John 15, 221
West, Christopher 222
Where the Rainbow Ends 102
Wiesenthal, Grete 126
Wilder, Thornton 76
Wilhelm 174
Wilkinson, Marc 130
Williams, Bill 216
Williams, Clifford 130
Williamson, Nicol 104
Wiltzak, Anatole 142
Winton, Harry 40
Wittop, Freddy 114, 198
Wood, J. Hickory 110
Woizikovsky, Léon 146, 148, 204,
    227
World of Art, The 14
Wyatt, Frank 181
Wynn, Arthur 86
Wynne, Esme 102
Wynyard, Diana 24

Young, Joan 76
Younge, Mr. 196
Yvain, Maurice 119

Zadek, Hilde 206
Zig 198
Zorich, George 158
Zverev, Nicolas 142, 146